Forgiveness
Learning How to Forgive

3rd Edition

Julia Frazier White, PhD
Illustrations by Cheryl A. White

Copyright © 2021 by Graham Lomas.

ISBN-978-1-6485-8066-6

All rights reserved. No part of this book may be reproduced or transmitted in any form or by any means, electronic or mechanical, including photocopying, recording, or by any information storage and retrieval system, without permission in writing from the copyright owner.

The views expressed in this work are solely those of the author and do not necessarily reflect the views of the publisher, and the publisher hereby disclaims any responsibility for them.

Matchstick Literary
1-888-306-8885
orders@matchliterary.com

I Forgive You

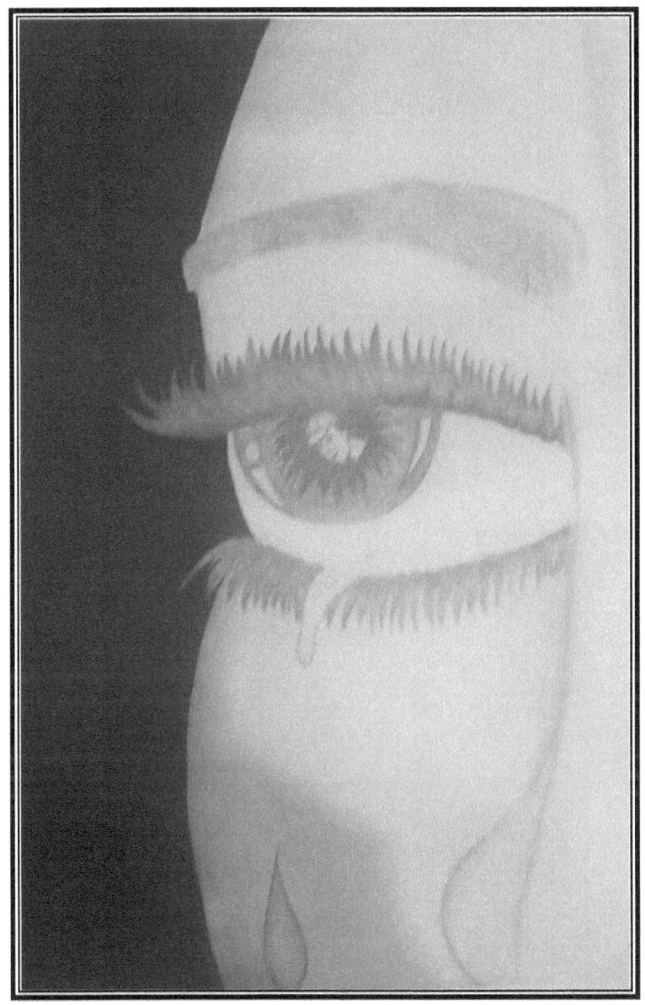

"I Forgive You"
Pencil and Charcoal Drawing by
Cheryl A. White

Contents

I Forgive You iii
Dedication vii
Abstract ix
Acknowledgments xi
Background and Definitions xiii
Prolegomena xvii

PART 1

Introduction 3
Chapter 1 11
Chapter 2 19
Chapter 3 27
Chapter 4 31
Chapter 5 39
Chapter 6 43
Chapter 7 51
Chapter 8 65

PART 2

The Forgiveness Process 73

PART 3

Ramona's Story 81
Jeannie's Story 87
Stella's Story 92
Chandler's Story 99

Allen's Story 101
Charley Mae's Story 102
Warren's Story 105
Gloria's Story 107
Andrew's Story 113
JoAnna's Story 118
Jennifer's Story 124
Alison's Story 125
From the Antwon Fisher Movie 131

Conclusion 133
Appendix A 135
Appendix B 139
Endnotes 151
Bibliography 155

Dedication

To my dear departed father, Latham Norvell Frazier,
for his gentle nature, his constant encouragement, and
his unconditional love and acceptance of me.

To my precious departed mother, Alyce Brewer Frazier, for
always loving me and teaching me so many things about life.

To my beautiful children, Richard Frazier White,
Anthony Brewer White, and Cheryl Ann White;
my daughters-in-law Mariessa and Aline.

My grandchildren, Lucas Antonio Romanini White, Sofia
Giulia Romanini White, and those soon to come.

To each of you who seek the peace of mind and the gift
of love that you can reach by learning to forgive.

He has taught us forgiveness and
the mighty power thereof.
He gave us the gift to undo things that
keep us from His love.

Julia Frazier White
The Power of Reversal

Abstract

Much of the existing literature on forgiveness speaks of forgiveness as a nice thing to do. Often the command to forgive is learned in early childhood and almost treated like a wonderful piece of prose. It is known as the Lord's Prayer, and it states that our debts (transgressions) will be forgiven by God as we forgive others.

In this manner, therefore, pray:
Our Father in heaven,
Hallowed be Your name.
Your kingdom come.
Your will be done
One art has it is in heaven.
Give us this day our daily bread.
And forgive us our debts,
As we forgive our debtors.
And do not lead us into temptation,
But deliver us from the evil one.
For Yours is the kingdom and the power and the glory forever.
Amen.[1]

The next two verses are more specific:

For if you forgive men their trespasses, your heavenly Father will also forgive you. But if you do not forgive men their trespasses, neither will your Father forgive your trespasses.[2]

These are very definite commands. The consequence of not obeying the command to forgive is stated in clear terms. If we do not forgive, then our heavenly Father will not forgive us. We would exist in a state of unforgiveness. Most people do not want that kind of existence. This study finds that people *want* to be in good standing with God and people, but many have indicated that they do not know *how* to forgive.

The findings in this book assert that having a step-by-step methodology will enable people to learn *how* to forgive and that once they experience forgiveness, the process becomes easier and easier. Eventually, the act of forgiving is internalized and becomes a life skill. Many of the people interviewed for this book have found that being free from the guilt and other burdens of unforgiveness means being free to love again. These interviews have been held in many venues with hundreds of individuals. This methodology has been taught in Sunday school, in nonreligious settings, and in private homes. The emphasis of this book is put on how individuals can learn to forgive. There is another powerful side of forgiveness—seeking to be forgiven. However, this book concentrates on teaching individuals *to forgive* because that seems to be the basis for all forgiveness in families, for nations, and the world. Again, by empirical determination, this study has helped persons gain peace—a peace that "surpasses understanding"—through forgiveness.

Acknowledgments

I am grateful for all the support I have received. I am especially thankful for my dear departed mentor and friend, Dr. David T. Shannon, Sr. The brilliance of this scholarly giant illuminated my path as a mentor, and I had to continue writing. Dr. Shannon read the early version of the manuscript and said that he would be delighted to write the foreword. We did not get to that point before death intervened. This book will not have a foreword.

I wish to thank Dr. Ora Cooks for her encouragement and help with formatting the book. Dr. Cooks has such vast knowledge, and she shares unselfishly. I eagerly took in her teaching as much as possible. Sometimes I felt like a deer in the headlights, and I thank her tremendously.

Thanks to Dr. Winston Lawson for reading the total manuscript and giving suggestions for the changes that have been incorporated in this book. Manuscript readers also included my daughter, Cheryl Ann White, and my sister, Marva Frazier Greene. I am so grateful for their offering corrections and insight.

Rev. Victor Williams was an early encourager who helped me decide what audience I wanted to address with this book. We discussed my ideas, and Rev. Williams said, "You have a heart for God. Go with your heart."

My sons Richard Frazier White and Anthony Brewer White periodically encouraged me to get finished writing so that this book could be read and used. Other members of my family too have been so encouraging: Cheryl Ann White; Jay and Rebeka Syberg Beach; Robert and Marva Frazier Greene; Joyce and Donald Stout; Ray Frazier; Delores Frazier, Evelyn Frazier Bates; Vanessa and Terry Humphrey; Vanetta Kyle; Dr. Aline Magnoni; Chhaya Kapadia; and Kenneth

Brewer Crawford. Several friends including Lennell Smith Wade, Samuel Cushman, Kathryn Stewart, Julia Alford Davis, C. Brandon Williams, Sherry Alford Robinson, Averett Shannon, and others listened and offered sincere encouragement so that I felt empowered to go on. Julia Alford Davis made a special trip to Atlanta to see how she could help me go forward. She looked at what I had written and commented, "You have written a book."

Background and Definitions

The Forgiveness Process was conceived over a period of time. It has been my experience that forgiveness is the answer to many of life's problems. The rewards of forgiveness are still being revealed through many avenues. The first mention of forgiveness in my life, to my knowledge, came through religion. It is the moral code of most of the world's religions to have people in good relationships with each other and in good relationship with God. An example of this point outside of Christianity is in Buddhism. When asked if being able to forgive one's enemies can make a difference to one's spiritual progress, the Dalai Lama answered, "Yes, yes, there is no doubt. It's crucial. It's one of the most important things. It can change one's life. To reduce hatred and other destructive emotions, you must develop their opposites—compassion and kindness. If you have strong compassion, strong respect for others, then forgiveness is much easier. Mainly for this reason, I do not want to harm another. Forgiveness allows you to be in touch with these positive emotions. This will help with spiritual development."[3] From the Hindu religion, we learn: "They tell us: do not be discouraged in seeing the failing of others. Rather, let it help awaken your understanding of them as to where they are in consciousness and the suffering they must be going through. If others harm you in thought, word or deed, do not resent it. Rather, let it awaken compassion, kindness and forgiveness. Use it as a mirror to view your own frailties, then work diligently to bring your own thoughts, words and deeds into line with Hindu Dharma."[4] Spiritual development is vital and is now being recognized in the counseling profession.[5]

Throughout most of the twentieth century, psychologists and other mental-health professionals were not sympathetic toward religion or spirituality. It was always a challenge, but the counselors could not give spiritual help when they themselves felt spiritually dry.[6] It may have been born out of a desire to separate church and state. As a result, society in general sets many of the tenets of religion aside in favor of the more socially acceptable and logical, non-cleric handling of those tenets. Slowly, it seems, we have come back to recognize the truths of life's moral code as being bigger than the religious "box" into which they had been relegated. Truth itself cannot be put into a box. It is too big for a box. It *is* the box. The separation of Church and State may apply to human relationships, but it does nothing to restore wholeness to the human being.

It is unhealthy for the human to be fragmented or divided into parts. The healthy human is a whole person - not fragmented. Forgiveness helps put the parts together again—mind, body, and spirit. The human being whose mind, body, and spirit are not operating together is often referred to as a "fragmented" individual. I have also heard the term "unbalanced" to describe this person, but I use the term "fragmented" because it seems to conjure a picture of brokenness more so that out of balance. I think fragmented people have fragmented thinking. They do not see the whole. To live well, I believe each of us must see ourselves as a whole person—mind, body, and spirit. In fact, *Roget's New Millennium*™ *Thesaurus* says that the word "wholesome" is an adjective that means "healthy" with synonyms such as "all there, together, fit, good, sane, sound, strengthening, virtuous, and well." The wholesome person is not fragmented. There is balance.[7]

Consider the fragmented person who is a mental giant (big mind) and a spiritual dwarf (little spirit). This person tries to handle everything intellectually. Therefore, the wounded spirit is not recognized. If the wounded spirit is not recognized, then they see no need to completely give up (forgive) any of the junk that affects (or infects) their spirit. They make such statements as, "It (the violation) didn't hurt me. I was just teed off." I have even heard the Mental Giant say such things as, "You shouldn't let it (the violation) bother you!" In other words, ignore the wounded spirit and pretend that the spirit has no value—only the intellect has value. As stated earlier, even today, many counselors fail to see or admit that there is a spiritual dimension to all human problems. Another part of the whole person is the body.

Consider the fragmented person who gives more attention to the body (physical well-being) than to the mind or the spirit. This person may handle a violation by trying to jog it off, body-building, extreme sports, or beating on something or someone. This person tries to handle everything physically—so much so that the wounded spirit is not recognized. If the wounded spirit is not recognized, then they see no need to completely give up (forgive) any of the junk that affects (or infects) their spirit.

Consider the fragmented person who is very "spiritual." This is the hard one to consider as being fragmented because, ideally, if one is spiritually healthy, then the rest falls in place. However, I am making a distinction between being spiritually mature and a so-called "spiritual" person. It seems to me that "spiritual" people consider themselves to be spiritually superior to others. The "spiritual" person does not even consider the rest of the person. When the spirit is wounded, the "spiritual" person can be heard making such statements as, "I'm waiting on Jesus" or "Let go and let GAUD" or "You should do such and such." This person cannot sit next to a certain person in church because of "what they did to me" ten years ago. The "spiritual" person seems to have a long memory for keeping up with infractions. They may even rehearse the infractions over and over. However, they do not recognize that their spirit is wounded. If the wounded spirit is not recognized, then they see no need to completely give up (forgive) any of the junk that affects (or infects) their spirit.

An out-of-balance person is fragmented in their approach to life. We need to be whole. We need to be healthy. We need our minds, bodies, and spirits to all function in balance. If there are things that happened in the past that throw us out of balance, we can use our power to forgive to help restore that balance. The bitterness and stress of unforgiveness is like a cancer to our emotions. The forgiver has mind, body and spirit to keep healthy. For health reasons, then, we would be better off with forgiveness.

I was one of those out of balance persons. I handled everything with my intellect. I lived with the stress of carrying all the hurts and fears from the present into the present. When I started to get emotionally and spiritually mature, I realized that I was living with unforgiveness and did not even understand forgiveness.

It simply is not enough to say that one *should* forgive. To fully embrace this life-changing principle, one must learn *how* to forgive. The purpose of this book is to do just that—offer practical, professional, and spiritual tools that can serve as a healing platform for those embarking on this important journey. Initially intended for me and my children, I found that sharing my testimony and the renewal I've witnessed through forgiveness to be nurturing to others and empowering to me. The immeasurable restoration to wholeness I have experienced has brought balance back to my life that allowed healing to take place in my life. I have become empowered enough to share the techniques that supported my path to forgiveness and renewal with others.

Prolegomena

In doing the research for this book, one person's story was so powerful that it is included here in preface to other powerful stories found in Part 3 – Using the Forgiveness Process. It still hurts to tell the story. After twenty-five years, our marriage came to an abrupt end. It was excruciating for all. Before the head-on collision, my husband had been a great family man, a generous man. He was an involved father: T-ball coach, Little League baseball coach, and soccer coach for each of our three children's teams. Each year he bought a packet of ten tickets to the Citi Symphony. When there was a concert featuring a violin piece, he took our daughter. She played violin in her junior and high school orchestras. If there were a concert featuring French horn, he took our sons. Each son played French horn and sat in first chair. The last five tickets were used for the entire family to attend a show by the Citi Symphony. He played tennis and was his league's "Over-35" men's tennis champion for State. He was a good neighbor and kept our house and lawn in excellent condition.

As a result of that horrible head-on car crash, the drunk driver died immediately, and my husband suffered horrific bodily injuries, including a severe head injury. Our family was never the same afterward. My husband had become a violent man given to fits of rage. He blamed everyone but himself for his actions. He had a different personality than before the head-on collision killed the drunk driver who wrecked into my husband on Interstate Highway 75. Through extensive microsurgery to transfer tendons, a useless arm and hand became viable again after physical therapy and occupational therapy. However, the head injury lingered and became worse over five years. The violence escalated. He knocked holes in the walls and doors. He was too big to hold. It was dangerous to touch him when he was in a rage. The children and I were afraid all the time. I put up a brave front, but I was frightened, too. Caught between trying to help him get back to normal and protecting the children from physical and emotional harm, I was weary.

Life became a series of police calls for help. There were several arrests, and each time it became harder to live with him upon his return. The volatility became unbearable. Then, one day, he started fighting our daughter and his niece because they had not done their laundry. I tried talking him down from the rage. His face was almost unrecognizable; his eyes were like vacant black holes from which came fiery glints. I said, "Let's talk about it. You just don't kill somebody about laundry." He became angrier and came after me. He said, "You took their side. I will break your damn neck. When the police get here, they will take me out of here, but you won't know a thing about it." That said, he jumped up from the table, pulled me up, and started choking me. I was so scared, but I did what the counselor had told me to do if he started pushing me or choking me.

For over two years, the counselor had told me, "Your husband is dangerous. If he becomes physically violent, you must not fight back because he is too big for you, making matters worse. It would be best if you were reflective. In a rage, he will not know what he is doing. Tell him what he is doing and ask if he means to hurt you." As his grip tightened, I kept repeating, "You have your hands on my neck. You're choking me. Do you mean to hurt me?" Not knowing what else to say or do, I repeated those phrases several times.

After calling 911, the girls were screaming, "Oh no! Dad, stop! Look at Mom's face. It's turning blue. Her eyes! Oh, no! Dad, stop!" They tried hitting my husband on his back with objects such as the heavy chrome kitchen chairs that just bounced off his back. I remember praying, "Please, God, do not let me die in front of my children." I started the reflective statements again. "You have your hands on my neck. You're choking me. Do you mean to hurt me?" Not knowing what else to say or do, after repeating the reflective statements several times to him, he stepped back and put both hands in the air, and his face returned to normal. At about that same time, the police came in and asked my husband, "What's going on?" My husband calmly said, "Nothing, buddy. Come in. Have a seat. I'm just trying to get these teenagers to do their laundry."

The police officers arrested him, took me and my daughter and his niece to the police station for statements, and took pictures of my neck. It was the last day my husband and I were together. I immediately changed the locks on the doors and changed the garage door combination in case the police let him come back home. I was so afraid that my head was buzzing with fear and pain.

A bitterly contested divorce, replete with stalking and harassing phone calls, followed. I took out restraining orders to keep my husband away from our home, our children's school, and my job as an engineer at a large company.

Our relationship was severed entirely, but I knew that I did not want to live with bitterness and cynicism for the rest of my life. I would have to forgive and teach my children to forgive. It was not easy. My children did not understand why they should forgive and why I would ask them to do so. I explained to them that it was for their mental, spiritual, and physical well-being. They were skeptical, and I kept talking with them about forgiveness. My greatest fear at that time was my children's ability to ever get past all the hurt and anger without becoming bitter and cynical young people. I found that it simply is not enough to say that one *should* forgive without teaching them *how* to forgive.

The purpose of this book is to help one know *how* to forgive. I started writing it for my own growth, but as I shared it with others, I saw healing take place in many lives. I wrote parts of *The Forgiveness Process: Learning How to Forgive* for more than two decades. It has been the experience of this author that forgiveness is the answer to many of life's problems. The rewards of forgiveness are revealed through many avenues. The first mention of forgiveness in my life, to my knowledge, came through my church attendance. It is the moral code of most of the world's religions to have people in good relationships with each other and a good relationship with God. It seems, however, in the effort to separate church and state, many of the tenets of religion were set aside in favor of the more socially acceptable and logical, non-cleric handling of those tenets. Slowly, it seems, we have come back to the recognition of the truths of moral code as being more prominent than the religious "box" to which they had been relegated. Truth itself cannot be contained in a box. It is too big for a box. It IS the box. The separation of Church and State may apply to human relationships but does not apply to human beings. It is unhealthy for the human to be fragmented or divided into parts. A healthy human is a whole person – not fragmented. Forgiveness contributes greatly to putting the fragmented pieces back together.

PART 1

Introduction

I know some things that have made a difference in my life and in the lives of those with whom I have shared. I know how to forgive and I went from being a person full of suspicion and fear to being a person full of power and love. As I share what I have learned, I have actually seen people change right before my eyes as they start to get released from the shackles of bitterness, hatred, loathing, and fear. I have watched attitudes change as people no longer felt like victims. Their countenance changed as they at last could genuinely smile. Their outlook on life changed as they were free to love—no longer bound by unforgiveness.

All these conclusions have come about through empirical observations, not mathematical, statistical, or clinical trials. I am a lay person who knows that forgiveness can make a difference in a person's life if they are willing to try it. I have seen it in my own life, and I have seen it in other people as I share with them in workshops, interviews, and speeches. I have spoken to church congregations, addressed private organizations, and corporate team meetings.

The goal of this book is to teach individuals to forgive so that they can move on with their lives. I have heard people say that they "should" forgive, but they feel that they just don't know *how*. People say that they are left very unhappy. They are angry, and anyone who reminds them of the person they don't forgive makes them angry all over again.

Over the past few years, I have talked with a number of people of all ages, races, and creeds. I have talked with Christians of many denominations, persons practicing Buddhism, the Bahá'í Faith, Judaism, and the Dharmic religions of Hinduism and Buddhism. I have talked with atheists. I asked each of them the question, "Do you think forgiveness will benefit you if you know how to forgive?" Most said that they want to forgive, but they are held back for various reasons. The most common reasons that have been stated to me seemed to be based on fear—fear that the perpetrator may "do it" to them again, fear that they (the victim) will forget what they want to remember, and fear that they might say they do forgive when they really don't forgive. Holding onto these fears is holding onto unforgiveness. The unforgiving heart is consumed with something negative. I feel that if people know more about forgiveness, then they will be more willing to forgive. I feel that to forgive, people need the answers to the following:

- What is Forgiveness?
- What Forgiveness is not.
- Why is Forgiveness needed?
- What is the Forgiveness Process?
- What is life like after Forgiveness?

Much has been written on the subject of forgiveness. Many people feel that there is a guilt piled on top of the need to forgive because they just don't know *how* to forgive. They say that they want to forgive but just don't know HOW to forgive. All of us have to deal with forgiveness from time to time. I have heard statements such as, "I know I should forgive her, but after what she did to me, I just can't. I'm afraid if I forgive her, she will do it again." One young woman who had been raped as a child said, "After what he did to me, I just can't forgive him. I can't let him get away with it." Like so many people I have talked with, this young woman thought forgiving seemed like something impossible that a lofty god sitting on high commands us to do. Unlike the famous saying, we don't seem to be able to "Just do it!"

Whenever I asked the question, "Do you want to forgive him or her?" the answer is varied. Some say a flat "No," while others say, "Yes, I want to be a forgiving person, but I just can't." Of course, there are the "I don't know" answers also.

But I find the hardest ones to deal with are those who say, "Oh, I forgave them a long time ago, BUT I won't forget it." This book will consider each type of reaction and look at how each person can successfully forgive even the vilest kind of offense. It doesn't matter where the pain came into one's life. It is crucial to be able to let go of the pain. Until one lets it go, the pain from unforgiveness is just a very heavy burden. We must move on. Our holding on to a violation may be more destructive than the original violation.

Relationships

Relationships will be mentioned throughout this book. Healthy relationships are beneficial to both parties in the relationship. I am referring to relationships as being one on one. In many settings, it may seem that there are numerous people in relationship to each other. However, if we go to the smallest common denominator, it will eventually become clear that each relationship is a one-to-one occurrence. I refer to each relationship as healthy or broken, horizontal, or vertical.

A *horizontal* relationship is person-to-person. A *vertical* relation is person-to-God. To my mathematical way of thinking then, there are four kinds of relationships, and for each, I will tell how I use the descriptions in this book. They are (1) Healthy Horizontal, (2) Unhealthy Horizontal, (3) Healthy Vertical, and (4) Unhealthy Vertical.

Healthy Horizontal

This kind of relationship is a people-to-people relationship that is based on a bond of trust. That bond of trust keeps the relationship healthy and allows it to flourish and grow all the way to love. The foundation of that love is sharing, trust, regard, respect, and intimacy. The healthy horizontal relationship is to be protected at all cost. Now, this doesn't mean that we should coddle each other. Trust is broken when we coddle, because most of the time when we coddle someone, we are pretending and at least one of us knows that it is a lie. If the other person doesn't know it, you know it and it eats at your insides. It leads to such thoughts as, "I should have said this or that" or "I was just trying to be nice." Another lie! "Nice" is good for nothing if it springs from a lie. Look at it like this: Your "trying to be nice" means that you don't trust the other person to respond to what you feel is truth in a way *you* can handle. So, you try to "be nice" just to keep up the *appearance* of love and trust. Say "good-bye" to the healthy relationship. When trust is gone, the relationship is no longer healthy. It is unhealthy, and you're the first to know. In the *healthy horizontal* relationship, we can confront each other in love.

Unhealthy Horizontal

This kind of relationship is a person-to-person relationship lacking in what each or both persons need from the other. Trust is missing. Love is missing. Intimacy is missing. These people do not enjoy being around each other. It may have been your decision to end the relationship, or it may have been terminated for you by a breach of trust, a misunderstanding, or from one person violating the other. It is especially hard if the relationship was at one time with someone you considered to be a trusted person in your life. In love, there is risk involved when we allow ourselves to be vulnerable.

When circumstances no longer allow for a bonding love, the relationship is broken. The original relationship may have been with someone close such as a family member or a friend. Feelings run all the way from hurt to bitterness, from loneliness to feeling totally isolated. The relationship is broken. In the case of our being violated by a total stranger, the relationship is broken. It is an unhealthy horizontal relationship. So, it doesn't matter how long we knew the person. When the relationship is broken, we have what I am calling an unhealthy horizontal relationship.

Healthy Vertical Relationship

No matter what your religious persuasion is, there is someone bigger than you. Some call that a "higher power" and some call it a "greater being." I call it God. This kind of relationship is a person-to-God relationship based on love and trust. In this relationship, we believe that God has our best interest at heart at all times. We trust Him. We love Him. God's love is so freely given to us. This relationship is based in truth too. We cannot fool God by our pretense of positive actions. We must be truthful with God at all times. Our being truthful with God means that we trust Him. We have faith in Him. Without faith, it is impossible to please Him.[8] We know that He loves us even when we don't deserve His love.

Unhealthy Vertical Relationship

This is almost a misnomer because when the relationship with God is unhealthy, we do not trust God to be there for us. We do not trust God to love us. The relationship is broken and would need to be restored before it is healthy again. When this relationship is broken, the person-to-God relationship is an unhealthy vertical relationship.

The "Broken" Relationship

Throughout this book, I refer to any unhealthy relationship simply as a "broken" relationship. I have been advised to tone down the description and say something like a "damaged" or an "impaired" relationship. But I like simplicity: I simply cannot envision an exquisite piece of crystal being described as damaged as it lays shattered on the floor after a fall. It is broken! However, unlike a fragile piece of crystal, through the miraculous power of forgiveness, relationships may be restored. In some cases, it is desirable for the relationship to be restored. However, the relationship doesn't need to be restored for forgiveness to take place.

When we look at the Forgiveness Process, we will see the importance of understanding the difference between forgiveness and restoration of the relationship. We will look at forgiveness in terms of what it is, what it is not, who can forgive, why forgive, the relationship between forgiving and forgetting, and life after forgiveness. We will examine the Forgiveness Process and look at some real-life stories of forgiveness.

Chapter 1

FORGIVENESS WHAT IT IS

*Forgiveness does not mean condoning what has been done.
It means taking what happened seriously . . . drawing out the
sting in the memory that threatens our entire existence.*

—**Bishop Desmond Tutu**

Chapter 1

FORGIVENESS—WHAT IT IS

> *"What if it were your mother getting beat every night?" Sheilah asked. "Would you still say that she should forgive the power freak who beat her until she didn't know who she was? Mother became like a walking zombie—always wondering what she could do to keep him from hitting her. After she finally left, you say she should forgive him? How?" Sheilah didn't even feel like she could forgive her father for abusing her mother all those years! "I just can't forgive that man."*

Sheilah came into work each day with an attitude of complaining. To the greeting of "Good morning," Sheilah typically said, "What's so good about it?" All those years of fear and anger had turned into cynicism and bitterness. Sheilah didn't think she could forgive her father. As a matter of fact, Sheilah was angry with her mother too and didn't think she could forgive her either. Before we can forgive, we must believe that we *can* forgive. We need to realize what forgiveness is, understand the power of forgiveness, and then we can realize the benefits that forgiveness brings to us. Like so many things in life, it comes to the point that forgiveness is a *choice* we can make.

We can hold onto the "stuff" that we took in from circumstances and incidents, or we can let it go—forgive. The choice is simple—hold onto the weight of unforgiveness or let it go. Although the choice is simple, it is not easy. Forgiveness is a *gift* you give to yourself. It is not something you do *to* or *for* someone else. Forgiveness is not even for the other person. It is for you! When we have not forgiven someone, it's just like we are carrying that person around with us. They are in control of our thoughts, and they control our responses to others in life. Many of the decisions we make in life are colored by the old tapes playing in our heads due to taking in "stuff" from the past events. Some things that happened may have been catastrophic events, highly traumatic perpetrations. Still, most happened to us over a period of time. Later we realized that we had been left with hurt, hatred, bitterness, self-hatred, jealousy, addiction to alcohol, drugs, food, sex, mean-spirited behavior, other destructive behavior, stress, depression, and other negativity. These negative things in our hearts and minds may have been caused by a number of things that happened to us such as:

- abandonment or neglect by parents,
- rape,
- physical abuse,
- emotional abuse,
- domestic violence,
- sibling rivalry,
- parents making a difference in children,
- being ridiculed and humiliated as a child,
- rejection,
- being lied on or having vicious rumors told on you,
- sexual molestation,
- intimidation and fear,
- unfaithfulness in marriage, and
- perceived wrongs (even if it is a mistake).

Unforgiveness dwells in our hearts, also, when we perceive that societal things, whether national or international, hurt us:

- systems of oppression such as racism and sexism,
- aggression that leads to war and strife,
- political polarization,

- wrongful persecution of another,
- historical misconceptions, and
- loss of loved ones in a war that we consider unjust.

The list can get very long. Each of us has a list of perpetrations. Our lists consist of anything that happened or that we perceive happened to us against our wills—overstepping our boundaries. It would be good if we could just try forgiveness and discover the benefits for ourselves. A television commercial for cereal a few years back said, "Try it. You'll like it." In the commercial, the older boys gave it to the youngest boy—who ate the cereal gladly. The older boys exclaimed in shock and disbelief, "He likes it!" Perhaps, then, the other boys will decide to try it. It's the same way with us when it comes to forgiveness.

Until we try it, we don't know the impact it can have on our lives. Until then, forgiveness is this intellectual matter. Once tried, we realize that forgiveness affects us in our minds and our bodies, and our spirits. It is a spiritual matter that can have physical effects on our bodies. The beautiful thing is that we don't really have to fully understand it to reap the benefits of forgiveness just like we don't have to fully understand the respiratory system to reap the benefits of breathing. Furthermore, just like breathing allows our bodies to release carbon dioxide, forgiveness allows us to release unhealthy "stuff" from our hearts and minds.

A simple definition of forgiveness is "release." It means taking the things out of your heart that weigh you down and letting them go! It means removing those things that cause you to have negative emotions (stress). That stress can cause not only emotional illness, but also physical and spiritual illness. Just like physical wounds need to heal, so do emotional wounds. The healing salve for emotional wounds is forgiveness. To heal, we must get rid of the anger, hatred, and bitterness that caused gaping wounds in our minds, spirits, and bodies. It is a gift that you can give anyone. More importantly, however, this gift may be the healthiest thing you can do for your own mind, body, and spirit. If we have been violated or feel that we have been violated, then there is a need to forgive.

A need to forgive certainly comes into being when there is a broken relationship. What is a relationship? What is a broken relationship? Some examples of broken relationships happen when you perceive that someone has done something against you. For example, you heard that someone said something about you that you don't think is true. You think the person lied on you. In actuality, it may not be a lie, but it is hurtful to you. Do you want to fellowship with the person that you think lied on you? Of course not! The relationship is broken. Before the relationship can be mended, the hurt must be removed from your heart, and the other person needs to do something to let you know that they did not mean to hurt you *and* that they will not do that again. To better understand forgiveness and to make it easier to forgive, we must separate forgiveness, however, from restoration of the relationship—reconciliation. Reconciliation is not always possible or even desirable. For example, you can forgive someone who has raped you or otherwise violated you, but your safety requires that you keep away. Or you may forgive the person who defaults on a loan but never again lend them money.

So, forgiveness does not necessarily mean the restoration of the relationship. Remember, we are commanded by God to forgive so that He forgives us, but we are not commanded to put ourselves in harm's way. We need to guard ourselves against physical, mental, and spiritual damage. This may mean allowing some relationships to remain broken even after the victim has forgiven the perpetration. Again, forgiveness does not necessarily mean the restoration of the relationship.

Restoration of the relationship (reconciliation) requires that both parties want the relationship to be restored and are willing to take the steps necessary to do so. While forgiveness can lay the groundwork for reconciliation, reconciliation requires more than just forgiveness. It requires that both parties consent to the restoration of the relationship (the reconciliation). Remember that in the broken relationship, trust is gone. It is only through true remorse and a demonstration of repentance (change of heart) on the part of the perpetrator that trust can be restored. Reconciliation, then, requires a forgiving victim and a repentant perpetrator. There is no reconciliation without repentance.

Until there is repentance, the relationship remains broken. Once we realize that reconciliation and forgiveness are different, then we are free to forgive—even forgive people who have died or have moved away from our lives. Forgiveness is for the forgiver!

In the Bible, Jesus Christ tells us to forgive others before we come to Him for forgiveness of our sins. Jesus wants us to have a pure heart and a clean mind so that we can appreciate life to the fullest extent. We cannot have that life with abundant happiness if we are constantly thinking about our perpetrators and the perpetrations—the things that I call "stuff." In the Christian faith, that negative "stuff" is called "sin," and it causes separation from God and neighbors. Can you imagine having a sack of "stuff" slung over your shoulders? It can get cumbersome! So, forgiveness is like taking "stuff" out of that sack. It is taking sin out of your heart—the sin that resulted from bitterness, hatred, and all other baggage. To keep these things in the heart is to live with unforgiveness. The emotional onslaught (stress) that results from unforgiveness can cause physical illness such as high blood pressure, depression, heart disease, stroke, heart attack, and other coronary events.

I saw a movie once called "Silence of the Lambs," and one line that I remember from that movie is, "You become what you hate." The molested becomes the molester. The hated becomes the hater. The deserted becomes the deserter. The abused becomes the abuser. If we forgive the acts of our offenders, then we can escape becoming victims of the offense. We escape being filled with bitterness and hatred. We have set ourselves free from the prison of bitterness and hatred.

Chapter 2

FORGIVENESS
WHY FORGIVE?

When a deep injury is done to us, we never recover until we forgive.

—**Alan Paton**, author of *Cry, the Beloved Country*

Chapter 2

FORGIVENESS—WHY FORGIVE?

> *Wanda and Lila had been friends for over twenty years. Gradually, Wanda noticed a change in Lila. Finally, Wanda asked, "What is it about you lately? We have been friends for a long time. Now you just try to make everything seem to be my fault. You never take my side anymore." Lila thought about this even after they got off the telephone. She concluded that her "friendship" with Wanda had been based on mutual hatred, bitterness, and general unforgiveness of the past. Childhood "stuff" lingered and languished because of continued rehearsal of the past. Lila had learned to forgive, and now her outlook on life was totally different. She was less judgmental and much more pleasant. Lila felt better and felt better about herself. She smiled more. She was still Wanda's friend but was no longer "brought down" by the past. They talked less frequently, but Lila loved Wanda more as she continued to love herself more.*

Wanda and Lila had been friends for years. Through the years, they constantly rehearsed their mutual pains. Childhood memories were often discussed in terms of how much each woman hurt. They compared their hurts, and each silently concluded that her own hurt was the greater. Each woman thought that no one else could understand, but it was just good to talk with someone about this "stuff" that each lived with. Fiercely competitive and very conscientious, each lived through years and years of professional success but negative emotional growth. Then Lila learned about forgiveness and started to grow in it. Lila's practice of forgiveness led to freedom in many ways and victory over many old hurtful times when she had looked at herself as a victim. As Lila learned more about forgiveness, she realized that there are many excellent reasons to practice forgiveness rather than live with unforgiveness.

There are so many good reasons to forgive. All point to one reason—to live in health. Through forgiveness, we maintain spiritual, mental-emotional, and physical health. We can become spiritually disabled as a result of resentment, bitterness, or anger. We can become mental-emotional cripples as a result of resentment, bitterness, or anger. We can lose our physical health to stress-caused diseases as a result of resentment, bitterness, or anger. It behooves us, then, to get rid of resentment, bitterness, and anger. Getting rid of such negativity is easier said than done. According to Dr. Simonton, forgiveness is part of a life-saving technique. He states, "Religious leaders of all persuasions and philosophers of every school plead the case for forgiveness. They wouldn't need to do so if forgiving were easy. But they also wouldn't suggest it if it were impossible."[9] No, forgiveness is not easy, but the rewards are manifested in our spiritual, mental-emotional, and our physical health. A lot of pioneering research is being done about forgiveness. It used to be relegated to religious sermons, not for scientific research. It has been known for a long time that forgiveness is better for you than holding a grudge. Dr. Hallowell, author of a book called *DaretoForgive*, states that toxic stress can be eliminated or reduced by forgiveness.[10] Dr. Hallowell also states that the most basic, proven reason to forgive is that chronic anger and resentment constitute a toxic form of stress and that toxic stress kills us much too young. He states that toxic stress leads to a multitude of physical and psychological problems. One is better off letting go of anger and resentment even if it were justifiable.[11]

Mental-Emotional Health

It has been proven in many studies that unforgiveness causes stress. Research and observations show that the person who forgives is a happier and healthier person than the one who does not forgive. When we carry unforgiveness, it is just as if we carry the other person with us everywhere we go. It affects our ability to trust people because we are not willing to risk being hurt again. Our hearts are full of whatever resulted from what somebody did to us or what we *think* they did to us. As a result, we have bitterness, hatred, unrest, mistrust, pain, and uneasiness. Wouldn't it be just wonderful to purge our hearts of all these negative, corrosive things—of unforgiveness?

Only recently has the science community realized the benefits of forgiveness. The value of these studies is that forgiveness will now be considered by many who otherwise considered it something that only "religious" people do. The first scientifically proven forgiveness program in this country was started by Robert D. Enright, PhD.[12] Dr. Enright shows how forgiveness can actually reduce anxiety and depression. His patients also experienced increased self-esteem and hopefulness toward one's future. Dr. Enright demonstrates how forgiveness benefits the forgiver and not necessarily the forgiven. Enright reassures readers that forgiveness does not mean accepting continued abuse or even reconciling with the offender. Rather, by giving themselves the gift of forgiveness, readers are encouraged to confront and let go of their pain in order to regain their lives. Others in the scientific community have realized the benefits of forgiveness, also. Dr. Enright, PhD, and Richard Fitzgibbons, MD tell of using the process of forgiveness in treating clients with psychotherapy.[13] Dr. Fitzgibbons cites these benefits to the one who forgives:

- decreased levels of anger and hostility,
- increased feelings of love,
- improved ability to control anger,
- enhanced capacity to trust,
- freedom from the control of events of the past,

- no longer repeating negative behaviors,
- improved physical health,
- significant improvement in psychiatric disorders.

Furthermore, Dr. Fitzgibbons states that one who cannot forgive may continue to suffer endlessly.[14]

There is widespread agreement that there is an emotional cost of refusing to forgive. If the perpetrator is someone the injured party must continue to see, each contact with the offender will cause the victim to feel upset again. When one continues to feel angry toward distant or dead perpetrators over transgressions that cannot be changed, it only makes the injured party stay miserable. Forgiveness would release the victim and would be a welcome relief.

Physical Health

Unforgiveness can have an effect on physical health. Recent studies have shown a definite correlation between stress and diseases such as cancer and heart disease. On January 2, 1998, ABC News reported, "Studies show that letting go of anger and resentment can reduce the severity of heart disease and, in some cases, even prolong the lives of cancer patients." Others, too, have told of the physically destructive nature of unforgiveness and bitterness.

In "Why Forgive?" Johan Arnold sites the actual experiences of ordinary people. He states, "Bitterness is more than a negative outlook on life. It is a destructive and self-destructive power. Like a dangerous mold or spore, it thrives in the dark recesses of the heart and feeds on every new thought of spite or hatred that comes our way. And like an ulcer aggravated by worry or heart condition made worse by stress, it can be physically as well as emotionally debilitating . . . and takes the ultimate toll on one's mind and body."[15]

Spiritual Health

One good reason to forgive is that we are commanded by God to forgive. We are told in scripture, "And whenever you stand praying, if you have anything against anyone, forgive him, so that your Father in heaven may also forgive you your trespasses. But if you do not forgive, neither will your Father in heaven forgive your trespasses," said Jesus.[16] This passage makes it very clear that our Father wants us to forgive. To not forgive, then, puts us in direct disobedience of this command. The Bible contains hundreds of references to forgiveness as important to our peaceful and loving relationships.

One of my favorite scriptures is Psalm 103. Here, we are told to "forget not" (remember) all the benefits of God, who forgives all your sins and heals all your diseases. Then there is the passage which states, "bearing with one another, and forgiving one another, if anyone has a complaint against another; even as Christ forgave you, so you also *mustdo*." [17] These are all compelling statements that reveal that forgiveness makes for better relationships with God and other people and will lead to more peace of mind. One can live with less stress and disease. There are compelling reasons to forgive.

Chapter 3

FORGIVENESS IS FOR EVERYONE

The weak can never forgive.
Forgiveness is the attribute of the strong.

—**Mahatma Gandhi**

Chapter 3

FORGIVENESS IS FOR EVERYONE

> *"Forgive? That stuff is not for me," said the street-wise Chuck. "That stuff is for you weak-minded religious types. I don't need to forgive. I just get even with anyone who crosses me." "Hey! What you lookin' at? Yo! Hey! Yeah, I'm talking to you! The last person who tried to stiff me got some of my brand of justice. Besides, I'm too smart to be bothered with all that weak stuff. You know what I mean? I mean I don't need to forgive nobody and I ain't gonna 'cause I need to keep up with who I can trust."*

Chuck does not believe that forgiveness is at all important. Forgiveness is for each person. It is not for the weak. It is for the strong. It is not just for the "religious" person. It is also for the atheist. It is not just for the Catholics. It is for every denomination. It is not just for the Democrats. It is also for the Republicans. It is not just for the store clerk. It is also for heads of state.

In his book titled *My Life*, past President Bill Clinton talks about not only forgiving his father, but also about reconciliation.[11] He states, "On those weekends, Daddy talked to me in a way he never had before. Mostly it was small talk, about my life and his, Mother and Roger, family and friends. Some of it was deeper, as he reflected on the life he knew he would be leaving soon enough. But even with the small stuff, he spoke with openness, a depth, a lack of defensiveness I'd never heard before. On those long, languid weekends, we came to terms with each other, and he accepted the fact that I loved and forgave him. If he could only have faced life with the same courage and sense of honor with which he faced death, he would have been quite a guy."[18]

Forgiveness is for the famous. For the Christian music band, the Katinas, learning that God was different from their childhood image led to a painful journey of understanding and forgiving their dad. From their Web site, http://thekatinas.com/, the group acknowledges that, "Our dad was a strict disciplinarian when we were growing up; it was a relationship born out of fear," Joe notes. "And when our mom died in 1988, there was a huge vacuum between us and our dad. We know that he has regrets, but we also know he did the best he could. In 1993 restoration and healing began—but it's still not always the easiest thing. Forgiveness is for the members of the band—any band."[19]

Forgiveness is for the man of God. A pastor who fell into an addictive pattern of adultery with members of three of the churches where he served as associate pastor was disciplined by the church according to scriptural direction. At the end of the period of discipline, that pastor addressed the church body. He said, "I'll tell you; it is really rich when you are obedient. I want to say again to any of you who are messing around in sin, let it go, give it up, ask God for forgiveness, and come back to the fold because therein lies true blessings and joy and peace."[20] Forgiveness is for everyone—even the pastor.

Chapter 4

FORGIVENESS
WHAT IT IS NOT

Forgiveness does not change the past, but it does enlarge the future.

—**Paul Boese**

Chapter 4
FORGIVENESS—WHAT IT IS NOT

> *My father raped me repeatedly for over fourteen years until I went away to college. I tried to talk with Mom about it. My mother shouted the angry words, "Yolanda, just try not to think about that anymore! It happened a long time ago. Your Daddy's dead now. I don't want to hear another word about it!" I needed to talk with somebody. How can I not talk about it with someone? Every night when he pressed his sweaty body on top of mine, I wanted to yell for Mom, but he said that if I told Mom he would kill both of us. It seems like Mom wants me to just sweep it under the rug like some left over dirt that will not go onto the dust pan. Out of sight is not out of mind. I live with painful memories of rape and bitterness toward him and my mother every day.*

Forgiveness Is *Not* . . . Easy

Forgiveness is not always easy. Forgiveness can be very difficult. This is especially in situations such as Yolanda's where she had been repeatedly sexually abused. "We need help in giving up feelings of revenge, in casting off feelings of hatred, and in being open to the possibility of a restored relationship."[21] Forgiveness is not easy. Just as you think you have mastered it in one part of your life, or in some of your relationships, "some new offense touches a deeply treasured piece of you, and hurt and anger flare again."[22] In the above example, Yolanda had anger and bitterness toward her mother as well as the perpetrator. Yolanda needed to be free from those bad feelings. That freeing process is known as forgiveness. We *must* forgive.

Forgiveness Is *Not* . . . Sweeping Things under the Rug

Forgiveness is not an act of sweeping things under the rug. Sweeping the last bit of dirt under the rug was never a good housekeeping technique. Soon enough, it will form a lump under the rug, and the constant wear will tear up the rug from the inside. Trying to sweep the abuse under the emotional rug was not a good technique either. Soon enough it will wear a hole in the heart and tear it up. Forgiveness will not allow things to be swept away. Instead, we must face our hurts, anger, and bitterness and express them and be rid of this negative trash once and for all. That cleaning process is known as forgiveness. We *must* forgive to live healthily and happily.

Forgiveness Is *Not* . . . Pretending

Forgiveness is not pretending that nothing happened, or that it did not bother us. We cannot hide from our past losses. We may think that we can hide our hurts from others. Most likely that is a myth also. A friend of mine tried for years to pretend that her divorce did not bother her. All the original hurts resurfaced, however, when her ex-husband announced to their grown children that he was getting married. All the anger that had been eating her up inside came to the surface. "How could he dare to bring that hussy to our family gatherings?" We cannot pretend the hurts are gone away. We must purge. That purging process is known as forgiveness. We *must* forgive.

Forgiveness Is *Not* . . . Minimizing the Loss

Forgiveness is not minimizing the loss. We may make statements such as "It didn't mean anything to me, anyway," but this does not mean that we forgave the perpetration. Minimizing or overlooking is not truly forgiveness. Here is an example of a statement that minimizes the infraction but does not indicate forgiveness: "Ah, I didn't like those gloves anyway."

One time I was robbed. Thieves broke into my car and stole my CB radio, some tapes, and some rare coins that I was taking to my new safety deposit box. At first, I tried to be stoic about the matter. I calmly went about reporting the event to the police, calling my husband, and reporting the loss to the insurance company. The insurance company really minimized my loss by valuing my rare coins at face value. I became very angry. In my anger, I realized that I had minimized the loss too. My loss couldn't be measured in material terms. No, my loss was greater than that. I felt violated! Those thieves had invaded my personal space and made off with a few of my personal possessions and a lot of my trust of mankind. We must not minimize our loss. It is better to face it square on and overcome it. That process for overcoming is known as forgiveness. We *must* forgive.

Forgiveness Is *Not* . . . a Sign of Weakness

Forgiveness is not a sign of weakness at all. It takes a strong person to face themselves and to understand their feelings. Once we understand or even allow ourselves to have the feelings that come up for us, we are on the road to emotional strength. We need to feel what we feel. Feelings can't be right or wrong—they just are. Forgiveness does not mean that we will allow ourselves to be doormats. In fact, forgiving means we have to set strong, healthy boundaries because we know how we want to be treated.[23] Our feelings, such as the gift of anger, let us know when our boundaries have been crossed.

Forgiveness Is *Not* . . . for the Other Person

Forgiveness is not for the perpetrator. It is for the forgiver. The other person may no longer be in your life. Furthermore, one may not want the other person to be in their life. Consider the most heinous crime of violation against one such as rape or murder of a loved one. Would you want that rapist or murderer in your life? I don't think so, unless there has been some reconciliation. You don't *have* to reconcile with the other person, unless it is mutually beneficial to do so. Now that we have established the fact that the other person may no longer be in your life, do you still want to live with the pain of that perpetration? Of course not! The other person is probably going on with his or her life, so carrying them around in your head and heart is weighing you down. Get rid of the excess weight—the stress, the pain, the bitterness, the ugly attitude.

Dr. Charles Stanley goes into detail to show that forgiveness is the act of releasing or setting someone free from an obligation to you that is a result of a perpetration done against you. He gives three reasons why forgiveness is for you, not for the other person! (1) The person who does not forgive is the loser. They live with an unforgiving spirit of bitterness. (2) An unforgiving spirit is a destructive force. Hostility from one relationship affects one's ability to get along with others. (3) When a person is hurt, often they feel rejected. That rejection and that resentment spill over into other relationships.[24] Excess baggage! Unload that baggage! That process of unloading the baggage is known as forgiveness. We *must* forgive.

Forgiveness Is *Not* . . . Automatic Restoration of Relationships

Forgiveness does not mean that a broken relationship is restored. Once a relationship is broken, it cannot be mended without the desire to do so by both the violator and the victim. I have heard children make such statements as, "I go with him, but he doesn't go with me." "He's my boyfriend, but I am not his girlfriend." "She is my friend, but I am not friends with her." These statements may sound like some childish descriptions of one-way relationships. Well, guess what? That's exactly right. Children have the clarity of vision to be able to see the relationship for what it is—one-sided. As adults, sometimes we do not like to admit that we are not in complete control of both sides of a relationship. The truth is we can only handle one side of the relationship. We can only handle our side. If the relationship is broken, there is nothing we can do to restore it without the involvement of the other person. Forgiveness does not automatically restore the broken relationship. As a matter of fact, we may not want to restore a relationship because of safety reasons or the threat of additional harm. We should never put ourselves in harm's way. For example, if one is raped, it is certainly not desirable or advisable to try to have a relationship with the rapist. It is important to forgive for the sake of healing from the pain, but a relationship with the rapist is not a good idea unless we know for certain that the rapist repents to us. How can we be certain? We cannot. We can, however, be certain that we do not want the rest of our lives controlled by the pains of the past. Forgive! We *must* forgive.

Forgiveness Is *Not* . . . Sanctioning Bad Behavior

Forgiveness is not condoning bad behavior. Behavior that is offensive to us must not be tolerated. We do not need to be codependents. There are many options when faced with bad behavior. One of the first options is to distance oneself from the behavior that we do not like. Another option is to try to get the offending behavior changed. One may even excuse the bad behavior and go on as if it never happened. This last option is in itself bad behavior, but it is a choice. Forgiveness does not mean that you allow anyone to wrong you over and over, and it does not mean that we condone or rationalize offenses.[25]

In summary, we do not have to tolerate bad behavior. Certainly, we do not need to sanction bad behavior. If we choose to forgive the offender, we still do not have to accept the behavior, and we can make that well understood. We may let it be known that we forgive the offender if that relationship is important enough for us to preserve. However, the important thing is to let go of any bad feelings we internalize because we don't like the behavior. Don't sanction it, but do free yourself from anger, bitterness, etc. Forgive! We *must* forgive.

Chapter 5

FORGIVENESS
FORGIVE AND FORGET

I can forgive, but I cannot forget, is only another way of saying, I will not forgive. Forgiveness ought to be like a cancelled note—torn in two, and burned up, so that it never can be shown against one.

—Henry Ward Beecher

Chapter 5

FORGIVENESS—FORGIVE AND FORGET

> *"There is no way I can forget what she did to me! It is just stupid to say that I should forget!" yelled Stan. Stan's best friend Jerry was trying to help Stan get over the fact that Trina had an abortion that ended the pregnancy. Stan felt that he should have been given more consideration and more say in the decision since he was the father. Trina told Stan that it was her body, so it was her decision. Stan cried, "Another body was involved too! Our unborn child had a body too, you know." Stan was inconsolable no matter what anyone said. He went into a mental and emotional tailspin and had to take off work to get himself together enough to cope with the great loss. He had hoped for a son. He vowed to never forget!*

The question comes up, "How can I forget? I will never forget it." It is true that intellectually one may not forget. Your memory banks are not erased by forgiving. However, your spirit is restored. You no longer have to live by the effects of that thing that robbed you of your peace of mind. So what we forget is the pain and the "victim consciousness" that came with the perpetration against you. Victim Consciousness is defined as "the conviction that someone else has done something bad to you, and as a direct result, they are responsible for the lack of peace and happiness in your life."[26] The event or infraction may always be part of our memory, but the pain associated with it is gone once we forgive that thing. Forgiving comes first.

Forgetting comes after forgiving. When we try to forget without forgiving, we may be successful in blocking it from our consciousness, but not from our memories. There have been cases where people years later "remember" something that happened to them. When it comes up to their conscious level of thinking, it is like it just happened all overagain. The pain from that perpetration had not been forgotten at all. It had been suppressed.

I knew a young woman named Mary who "remembered" in counseling that she had been molested by her older brother when she was three and four years old. She was devastated—especially when her older sister confirmed that her memories were accurate. Mary confronted her brother who confessed that he did indeed rape her many times when their mother went to the store. Eventually, Mary was able to forgive the violation caused by her brother, and she was able to forget the pain caused by the violation. However, she did not want a restored relationship with him for fear that he would molest her children too.

Often, we are told to "forgive and forget." This sounds like an impossibility. Perhaps it would be easier to understand if the expression "forgive and forget" could be stated "Forgive so that you can forget the hurt, anger, bitterness, and other destructive forces." Forgive so that you may forget the effects of the perpetration (i.e., pain), but you probably will never forget the event. There is no forgetting of the pain and other negative emotions without forgiveness. Forgiving comes first. We *must* forgive!

Chapter 6

FORGIVENESS
FORGIVING ONE'S SELF

He that cannot forgive others, breaks the bridge over which he himself must pass if he would ever reach heaven; for everyone has need to be forgiven.

—George Herbert

Chapter 6

FORGIVENESS—FORGIVING ONE'S SELF

> *I should have told Mom or Dad the truth, but my brother Brad asked me not to tell. Now Brad lies cold and still on a slab in the county morgue. The medical examiner said that Brad probably did not know what hit him and that he died immediately. I can't help but think, however, that I should have told Mom or Dad that Brad was planning to party with the crowd that Mom and Dad had warned Brad about. They may have stopped him so that he would not have been in that fatal wreck on his way back home. I just can't forgive myself for not telling someone about Brad's drinking and doping with his buddies.*

Tommy was two years younger than Brad, and he really looked up to his brother. Brad was headstrong and determined to live life his way. Brad and Tommy shared a room, but they did not share the same approach to life. Brad was smart and popular in school, but he decided to run with the wrong crowd. He succumbed too much to peer pressure. Tommy, on the other hand, was a good student, an athlete, and a very obedient son. When Tommy saw Brad preparing to go out that Friday night, he simply asked if he could go too. Brad did not like his little brother cramping his style with his "cool" friends, so he told Tommy who would be at the party and that he probably would not like the people there. Tommy knew the crowd of kids that Brad was going with and knew that Mom and Dad did not like Brad hanging out with them.

Brad asked Tommy not to tell who would be giving the party. Tommy kept Brad's secret until the phone call came asking the family to come identify Brad's body. Tommy blamed himself and kept saying that he just couldn't forgive himself. He wished he had stopped Brad somehow. It was painful enough to lose his brother, but to lose him under these circumstances was very disturbing to Tommy. His counselor reminded him that it had been Brad's decision to go to that party and to remember that accidents happen every day. Nothing relieved Tommy of the guilt and turmoil inside. He should have helped his brother stay away from that rowdy crowd even if it meant "ratting" Brad out to their parents. After counseling, Tommy still said that he just couldn't forgive himself. The youth leader from Tommy's church talked with Tommy about asking God to forgive him for helping Brad to disobey their parents.

I've heard many people, like Tommy, say, "I just can't forgive myself." This raises a question in my mind. I think, "if you believe God, then why must you forgive yourself? Simply ask God to forgive you. *Believe* He will because He said He will. Repent, so that you acknowledge that what you did was wrong and you will not do it anymore. Mean it!

Repenting simply means "turning around" or doing an about face. Now, if God forgives you, what more do you need? Do you need to improve on what God did? Or do you not believe God forgave you? You think you can do it better than God? I really think that the statement "I just can't forgive myself" means that we are bypassing God to try to do what He easily does if we humble ourselves to Him. "I just can't forgive myself" means that I have some guilt or other bad feelings about something I did. However, if we believe God, then we believe that "If we confess our sins, He is faithful and just to forgive us *our* sins and to cleanse us from all unrighteousness."[27] If God cleanses us from all unrighteousness, then what's left for us to forgive? Nothing! Nada! We simply need to ask Him and believe Him. God is the only One who can help people truly forgive and to go on.[28]

In talking with persons who said they can't forgive themselves, I concluded that some have not really admitted that they did something wrong to or against another. They seem to think that they have hurt nobody, or that they only affected themselves. As a result, they live with the disturbing thoughts associated with the perpetration. Just as sometimes we need to forgive others, sometimes we need to humble ourselves and ask others to forgive us. We do not need to live with unforgiveness. One author states, "Forgiving oneself means to experience the love that keeps no record of our own wrongs."[29] We must love ourselves as we love others and accept the forgiveness from others and from God.

A cute little story that was sent to me by a friend on the Internet illustrates what it means to live with unforgiveness. The story is called "The Devil and the Duck," and it illustrates the pain of living with unforgiveness and the need to be forgiven by someone. In this story, Johnny needed to ask his grandma for forgiveness. Because he didn't seek forgiveness, Johnny's sister was able to exploit Johnny's guilt and shame.

—OriginalInternetMessage—

The Devil and the Duck

There was a little boy visiting his grandparents on their farm. He was given a slingshot to play with out in the woods. He practiced in the woods, but he could never hit the target.

Getting a little discouraged, he headed back for dinner. As he was walking back he saw Grandma's pet duck. Just out of impulse, he let the slingshot fly, hit the duck square in the head, and killed it. He was shocked and grieved.

In a panic, he hid the dead duck in the wood pile, only to see his sister watching! Sally had seen it all, but she said nothing.

After lunch the next day Grandma said, "Sally, let's wash the dishes." But Sally said," Grandma, Johnny told me he wanted to help in the kitchen." Then she whispered to him, "Remember the duck?" So, Johnny did the dishes.

Later that day, Grandpa asked if the children wanted to go fishing and Grandma said, "I'm sorry but I need Sally to help make supper." Sally just smiled and said, "Well that's all right because Johnny told me he wanted to help." She whispered again, "Remember the duck?" So, Sally went fishing and Johnny stayed to help.

After several days of Johnny's doing both his chores and Sally's he finally couldn't stand it any longer. He came to Grandma and confessed he had killed the duck. Grandma knelt down, gave him a hug, and said, "Sweetheart, I know. You see, I was standing at the window and I saw the whole thing. But because I love you, I forgave you. I was just wondering how long you would let Sally make as lave of you."

Thought for the day and everyday thereafter: Whatever is in your past, whatever you have done—and the devil keeps throwing it up in your face (lying, debt, fear, hatred, anger, unforgiveness, bitterness, etc) whatever It is, you need to know that God was standing at the window and He saw the whole thing, He has seen your whole life. He wants you to know that He loves you and that you are forgiven. He's just wondering how long you will let the devil make as lave of you. The great thing about God is that when you ask for forgiveness, He not only forgives you, but He forgets—It is by God's Grace and Mercy that we are saved. Go ahead and make the difference in someone's life today. Share this with a friend and always remember...God is at the window!

It's a great little story illustrating how living with the pain of unforgiveness makes us a slave to sin. Break free! Learn to ask for forgiveness. Then just do it! Try it. You'll like it. You can be free from that burden of unforgiveness. In the story above, Johnny lived with the pain of unforgiveness simply because he had not asked for forgiveness. I feel that whenever we feel that we just can't forgive ourselves, it is because we are looking to the wrong person for the forgiveness. I feel that whenever we are living with the need to be forgiven, we must go to the person we have wronged to seek forgiveness. Remember too that when we have wronged another person (whether they know about it or not), then we have disobeyed some of the commandments that God gave us so that we might be in good relationships with each other. Two of the commandments that God gave us are to love one another and to bear one another's burdens.[30]

On the subject of loving one another, the scripture tells us to "Owe no one anything except to love one another, for he who loves another has fulfilled the law."[31] In other words, if we love one another, we will fulfill the law of love because we will not steal from them, lie on them, kill them, or covet their possessions. So, when we have wronged one another, we are operating outside of God's provision of loving relationships to each other and to God. The One we need to seek forgiveness from, then, is not only that person we have wronged, but we need also to ask God's forgiveness for going against what God wishes for us. I found it easier to keep the commandment to love others when I came to the realization that this does *not* mean that I have to *like* the person or their ways.

Another commandment given by God to tell us how to be in right relationship with each other is the command to bear one another's burdens: "Bear one another's burdens, and so fulfill the law of Christ."[32] If I see that you have a need that I can help you to meet and I withhold my help in the hopes that you will somehow fail, then I have done wrong according to the commandment of God. You may not even know that I wished any malady on you. However, I am now living in disobedience. I may feel guilty and think that I need to forgive myself. Actually, I committed the perpetration against God's command. I need to ask God to forgive me. Then I do not need to forgive myself. There's nothing left to forgive. There is no need to improve upon what God has done. To put it another way, there is no need to clean up after God. We have a choice: we can accept God's forgiveness with gratitude and a new attitude toward all.

Chapter 7

FORGIVENESS
THE NEED TO
RECEIVE FORGIVENESS

I think it means . . . putting yourself in the position of the other person, and wiping away any sort of resentment and antagonism you feel toward them.

—**Jimmy Carter,**
Thirty-ninth President of the United States of America
Nobel Peace Prize winner, 2003

Chapter 7

FORGIVENESS—THE NEED TO RECEIVE FORGIVENESS

> *The need to receive forgiveness is a strong, very real need. When we come to the conclusion that we have hurt someone OR we know that someone perceives that we have hurt them, there is a natural tendency to want to restore the relationship. As has been mentioned before, there is no restoration of the broken relationship without forgiveness and repentance. The person who feels victimized by us is not likely to want to be victimized again. We have no way back to them without their forgiving us. Of course, it is their choice whether or not they forgive us, but we can certainly ask for forgiveness. We must swallow our pride and go to the person whom we ostensibly have hurt. When we go to the "victim" and ask their forgiveness, it is just as if we have issued them an invitation to forgive us. We are seeking forgiveness.*

The seeking of forgiveness is from someone we feel that we have hurt or from one who has expressed that they perceive that we have hurt them in some way. Seeking forgiveness involves experiencing feelings of guilt and remorse and the desire for restitution. It comes from a contrite heart. It is not enough to say "I'm sorry." To truly seek forgiveness from someone, there must be the desire to right a wrong. There will also be a desire for restitution. Much has been written on this subject (i.e., Alcoholics Anonymous. Suggested steps for the seeking of forgiveness include the following:

- Admit you have wronged someone or that they perceive that you have wronged them. They feel victimized by you or you feel that you have victimized them.
- Decide to clear your conscience. How would you feel if the tables were turned?
- Choose an effective way to ask for forgiveness. Saying "I'm sorry" is not the same as asking for forgiveness. In fact, it's not asking for anything. Rather, it's telling something—something that usually has no real effect. People have been heard to say "I'm sorry" or "I'm sorry that you feel that way." Both statements sound fine on the surface, but neither statement indicates that they took any responsibility for what happened. It simply says that you are responding to what happened. This will not let the other person know anything about what might happen if the same situation occurs again. Will it be handled the same way or differently?
- Establish a promise of change. Ask forgiveness and state that you will not do that thing again. Your stating that you will not do that again is an act of repentance. It is an about face from where you were before. It is turning away from prior actions or way of handling things. It may reestablish the person's trust in you. There may be restoration if the person also desires restoration.

Let us look at a situation that illustrates seeking forgiveness. This is an overly simplified example. It illustrates the point.

Example:

Joan is standing on the sidelines after a high school football scrimmage game. Two young men decided to horse around by tossing the football. One young man, Ted, jumped up to catch the ball, lost his balance, and came down hard on Joan's leg and foot. Joan's ankle was hurt very badly by the weight of his body and the roughness of his cleats. Joan had to have emergency treatment for her ankle. The young man who ran into Joan said, "I'm sorry." Of course, he was very sorry, but Joan's foot continued to hurt. Just saying "I'm sorry" does not stop the pain. The pain must be dealt with by the person with the pain. As soon as the incident happened, the relationship between Joan and Ted was no longer bystander and student football player. That relationship immediately changed to victim and perpetrator. It does not matter that Ted did not mean to hurt Joan. The fact of the matter is that Joan was hurt. She could have chosen to be forever angry with Ted or forever be afraid to stand close to him in case he becomes careless again. Joan no longer trusted Ted not to hurt her foot. Ted could have opted to assume no responsibility for what happened. For example, he could have said that Joan was simply at the wrong place at the wrong time. He could have said that Joan should have watched out for herself. These statements may very well be true, but they do not help Joan and Ted want or trust being around each other too closely. The relationship is altered. It is broken because trust is gone. If there is to be restoration of the relationship, there must be a promise of change. Another word for this promise of change is "repentance." Ted repented to Joan.

There needs to be repentance so that the "victim" (Joan) can start to trust that the "perpetrator" (Ted) recognizes and respects her (Joan's) feelings and will do what can be done to protect her right to those feelings. Experiencing forgiveness and extending forgiveness to others, as Ted is inviting Joan to do, "can have a major impact on people who experience guilt. Forgiveness brings greater physical and mental health, heals racial and cultural divisions, restores marital stability, and builds relationships."[33] Ted did not want to be left with feelings of guilt. He asked Joan to please forgive him.

Ted might have said something like "Joan, please forgive me for running into you like that. I wasn't looking at where I was going. I will not horse around again like that when I am so close to other people. Please forgive me." This request for forgiveness means that Joan is being asked to do something.

Now it is Joan's turn for action. She can accept Ted's plea for forgiveness and acknowledge to Ted that she forgives him. She also could choose not to be forgiving—choose to stay angry. It's up to her. If she forgives Ted, she also may start to trust that this kind of accident will be very unlikely from Ted because Ted stated that he would not horse around so carelessly again. He gave a promise of change. Ted repented to Joan.

On the following pages, there are several more stories. The source of these stories is real life. Many people in these stories are ones with whom I have talked over the years. Some have been in national and international news stories. Each story illustrates our need to be forgiven. Perhaps you will see yourself in one of the following stories and will be led to seek forgiveness and even reconciliation.

Need for Forgiveness—Jill, the Other Woman

Jill relates her story: "I was the other woman. It started innocently enough. We were both hard workers and dedicated to getting the job done. Often, we stayed late to finish what did not get done during normal working hours. We attended conferences together. During late night dinners and after work drinks, we discovered that we really liked being together. We talked about everything. His wife did not understand him. My husband was not attentive. My husband hung out with friends whom I did not trust. This went on for a period of two years. Oh, how good it made me feel to have the attention from my lover. Even when I learned that his wife was complaining of the lack of time spent with her and their three children, I just felt sorry for him for being badgered by his wife.

"My husband was so inattentive that he did not notice. If he did notice, he was mighty quiet about it—not accusing at all. Well, he did travel quite a bit. So, he was out of town quite a bit. I was on speaking terms with his wife, so when I called their house to speak with him, she passed the phone or took a message. When he answered the phone, we spoke in coded terms so as to not be detected. After each call, he would find a way to call me in private. Not only was the conversation good, but the sex was even better! We had several meeting places—always romantic settings, always out of the way of either of our families. He made me know the joy of being romanced completely. He told me things that made me melt in his arms. He melted into me. We had all kinds of sex acts—each a successful experiment resulting in pure ecstasy. This climactic joy was totally different than what I got at home.

"Then there came a big blow! His wife asked him for a divorce. Naturally, I felt sorry for her, but I could not say anything to her about the affair. She even asked me if I knew what she could do to save her marriage. I gave her my best advice. I was not about to divorce my husband for this amorous, younger man with all those children. It was essentially over. He got a promotion in his job, and they moved away. We still talked, and when he came to town, we saw each other for dinner, but now as friends not lovers. I was guilt-ridden about the troubles he and his family were having.

"I wanted to be forgiven. However, I needed to be forgiven by the wife. I needed her to know, even though I thought she already knew because of the amount of time her husband spent with me, talked about me, and compared her to me. Still, I needed to be forgiven by her. A few years went by. There were times that he came into town, and I was too busy with my schedule or my husband. My husband and I had reconciled our differences and he gave me more of the attention that I felt that I needed. Then, one day, she called me. It was a friendly call, and I enjoyed talking with her. Most of all, I was just glad she called. I did not want to confirm the affair with her husband for fear of really hurting her to the core. I simply enjoyed our conversation and hung up happy. I had taken her call as forgiveness. I needed that forgiveness so much! I resolve to never again fall into adultery. It creates for me too great a need to be forgiven. I'm so glad she called me. In some way, I feel forgiven because she does not appear to be hurt. I hope this is so. I am reminded of a passage of scripture in the Bible that states that our real sin is against God. It states, 'Against You, You only, have I sinned, and done *this* evil in Your sight—That You may be found just when You speak, *and* blameless when You judge.'[34] My sin was against God. I am now sorry that I did something to another person that I did not want done to me. I have asked God to forgive me."

Need for Forgiveness—The Murderer

Jennie's mother recounted this story on television: "I witnessed his being sentenced to death for killing my daughter. Inside, I felt vindicated, but still empty. Oh, how I miss my daughter and the future we had planned for her. Jennie was only nineteen years old, vibrant and pretty. She had chosen to go away to college. I missed her and looked forward to her coming home during breaks in the school year. I missed her, but it was nothing like the hole left in my heart after her death. Knowing that she would never return seemed to have created a gigantic hole in my heart the size of the Grand Canyon. God, how I hurt!"

"I was also so very angry at the young man who had taken Jennie's life. His name was Pruett, and he was a drug addict and twice-convicted bank robber. He was imprisoned in the penitentiary in Atlanta. In 1978, he told officials there that he witnessed the murder of his cellmate then testified against the supposed killer. Pruett's testimony gained him freedom and admission to the witness protection program. Years later, he told police officers in New Mexico his story was a lie; that he actually did the killing and accused someone else in an elaborate plan to get into the program. Once in the witness protection program, Pruett went on a cross-country rampage, robbing banks in Bridgeville, Pennsylvania, and several other cities. He also killed at least five more people before he was caught in 1981. Marion Pruett gave himself the name 'mad-dog killer' who went on a murder spree while he was in the government's witness protection program."

(Read entire story at: http://www.prodeathpenalty.com/Pending/99/apr_execlist.html.)

Before the chemicals are released into the inmate's veins, the warden asks the individual if they want to say any last words. It is usually an expression of love for family and some kind of religious prayer or asking forgiveness. Marion Albert Pruett was executed in Arkansas. He asked God and his victims for forgiveness. As he was injected, he stated, "I would also like to ask all the people that I ever hurt, and their family members, to forgive me for all the pain," he said. "And I forgive everybody for what's about to happen to me."[35]

Kenneth B. Harris

"By the time Vicki Haack arrived at the 'Death Chamber' viewing room last Tuesday, the man who had murdered her sister Lisa was already hooked up to the intravenous tubes. In 1986, Kenneth B. Harris, a crack cocaine addict, had entered her sister's apartment, raped and choked her, and then spent an hour drowning her in her bathtub. Harris showed no fear. He turned his head to the side to smile and nod at his audience.[36] With the warden at his head and the prison chaplain at his feet, Harris said, 'I would like to thank all of you for coming. I am sorry for all of the pain I have caused both families—my family and yours. I would like for you to know that I am sorry for all the pain I caused for all these years. I have had time to understand the pain I have caused you.' With this statement, Harris was asking forgiveness. Then he told the warden he was ready to die. After the execution, Vicki Haack said that her family had forgiven Harris. 'We have no hate or bitterness in our hearts,' she said. 'But that doesn't mean he does not pay for his crime.' Not all murderers ask for forgiveness. Some are defiant all the way to death."

Need for Forgiveness—Siblings

Connie died of a massive heart attack at age thirty-four. She had undergone a series of operations to repair her ailing heart. Neither the angioplasty nor the bypass surgery was enough to save Connie. After suffering a stroke, then a heart attack, Connie gave up life as we know it. She died three days before Christmas. Her funeral was the following Saturday at eleven o'clock in the morning. As the family came into the small church, one of the sisters was heard to wail, "Connie wake up! I'm so sorry." You just knew there was some unsettled business between those two siblings. This was confirmed later during the dinner prepared by Connie's church family. Connie had been active at her church, regularly attending bible studies and church services. She was very talented in many ways but always seemed to be trying to find some answers to her unstated problems. She was a hard worker on her job.

Customers at the store where she worked seemed to like her because of her helpful ways and her genuine smile. The sister with the grievance against Connie kept crying very loudly during the funeral service. It was obvious that she was hurting so much. She kept saying, "Connie! I'm so sorry!" She had a need to be forgiven by Connie. I don't know what caused the rift between these siblings, but I do know that it was too late to ever restore that relationship. We can only hope that Connie did not hold the same kind of animosity toward her sister.

The need to be forgiven sometimes seems so great that a large amount of stress is created by the aching heart. If only that sister had realized this before Connie died, she could have made peace with Connie. There will be no reconciliation for the two sisters.

It is never too late, however to get relief from the unforgiveness. Prayer is a good way to get rid of unforgiveness. Ask God to take away the pain and resolve to never let that kind of bitterness be held in your heart again. There was a popular song a few years ago titled, "In the Living Years" where it is said to be too late when we die to admit we don't see eye to eye. It's too late to mend that relationship, but it is never too late to seek forgiveness.

Need for Forgiveness—The Abortion

Martha was sixteen years old when she got pregnant. At first, she could not believe what was happening to her body. Her mother noticed Martha's symptoms and suspected the truth. A trip to the doctor in the next town confirmed the situation—Martha was indeed pregnant.

When confronted with the facts, Martha's mother and father decided that Martha was not to tell anyone and that there would be an abortion.

The abortion counselor told Martha and her parents that they had come to the clinic just in time because there was no baby formed yet—it was just a blob of tissue. The abortion was scheduled. Later, after the abortion, Martha felt relief and felt that her life would return to normal. After all, the unwanted pregnancy was over, and her family was not embarrassed. What a relief! This relief did not last long, however. When Martha thought more about the abortion process, she thought, "Something powerful just happened in my body." The more Martha found out about abortion, the more she came to feel that she had killed her unborn child. She became depressed and bitter.

Years later, Martha got married to a wonderful professional man much like her father—professional in his job and controlling at home. To this union, two beautiful daughters and a son were born. It was during these pregnancies that Martha came to the conclusion that the first "blob" was a baby too. She felt very depressed and guilty. She was also angry at her parents for making her get the abortion. Martha always remembered the would-be-child's birthday and grieved.

After realizing the source of her grieving, Martha decided to get forgiveness. It, naturally, could not come from the unborn child, but she would ask God to forgive her. She faced her grief and prayed for forgiveness. In the process, she also forgave her parents for the roles they had played. She no longer blamed them for not telling her about the after effects of abortion. She decided that they must have thought they had done the right thing for their family. Martha wished she had stuck up for her baby, but she decided to let go of the bitterness and depression. Facing these feelings and celebrating the lives of the three children she had given birth to helped Martha feel that she had been forgiven.

Need for Forgiveness—The Lynchman

In a recent documentary on television, I learned of the lynching of a young man named Michael Donald. The heinous murder took place on March 21, 1981. Michael Donald was born in Mobile, Alabama, in 1962. Upset members of the Ku Klux Klan went looking for a black man to kill after a black man was acquitted for the murder of a white man. At a meeting held after that trial, Bennie Hays, the second-highest ranking official in the Ku Klux Klan in Alabama said, "If a black man can get away with killing a white man, we ought to be able to get away with killing a black man."[37]

On Saturday, 21 March 1981, Henry Hays and James Knowles decided they would get revenge. They traveled around mobile in their car until they found nineteen-year-old Donald walking home. They forced him into their car. Donald was taken into the next county where he was brutally lynched.

In June 1983, Knowles was found guilty of violating Donald's civil rights and was sentenced to life imprisonment. Six months later, when Henry Hays was tried for murder, Knowles appeared as chief prosecution witness. Henry Hays was found guilty and sentenced to death.

After a long-drawn-out legal struggle, Henry Hayes was executed on 6 June 1997. It was the first time a white man had been executed for a crime against an African American since 1913.

James Knowles, the lynchman, had a need to be forgiven. He said, "I've lost my family. I've got people after me now. Everything I said is true. I was acting as a Klansman when I done this. And I hope people learn from my mistake. I do hope you decide a judgment against me and everyone else involved." Then he turned and said directly to Beulah Mae Donald, mother of Michael Donald, "I can't bring your son back. God knows if I could trade places with him, I would. I can't. Whatever it takes—I have nothing. But I will have to do it. And if it takes me the rest of my life to pay it, any comfort it may bring, I hope it will."

Beulah Mae Donald gave a quick answer. She said, "I do forgive you. From the day I found out who you all was, I asked God to take care of you all, and He has."

Need for Forgiveness—The Down Low

Tim told his story of climbing back from the "down low": "I had a wonderful wife who loved me and our two little girls very much. I was on the 'down low' throughout most of our marriage. Men who discreetly have sex with other men while in sexual relationships with women are said to be on the 'down low.' Most of these men do not consider themselves gay or bisexual. Their female partners are not even aware that they have sex with men. I don't consider myself to be gay. It's just that I like having sex with other men. Quite frankly, a woman cannot compete with another man for sex. The reason I need to be forgiven is that now my wife has HIV. My God! I did not want that to happen to her. I love her, and I am so sorry that I brought this malady into our lives. When I look back, I can see that I was led by lust, not love. In my mind, I was a married man. In the flesh, I was a lustful man with a large sexual appetite. I had a strong mind but I had a weak flesh."

We are cautioned about the weakness of the flesh in the scripture that says, "Watch and pray, lest you enter into temptation. The spirit indeed is willing, but the flesh is weak."[38] This was certainly the case with Tim. Tim was remorseful and knew that he needed forgiveness.

"How can I be forgiven? I need my wife's forgiveness and I need God's forgiveness. I have hurt both. I have broken the relationship with my wife, but I broke the relationship with God even before that. I'll go first to God. Knowing that there is no restoration without repentance, I must first fix it in my heart and mind that I will not continue in the same destructive behavior. I must do an about face and turn away from the infidelity and away from the gay lifestyle. Who called it 'gay' in the first place?"

Chapter 8

FORGIVENESS
LIFE AFTER FORGIVENESS

If we really want to love, we must learn how to forgive.

—**Mother Theresa**

Chapter 8

FORGIVENESS—LIFE AFTER FORGIVENESS

> *After I learned to forgive, I realized a freedom that I had not known before. Even when things happen that would have bothered me before, I have learned to forgive faster—before I take in somebody else's "stuff" into my heart. Recently, at a church retreat, a member greeted me by saying, "Well, I see you haven't grown. You're so short. I like being tall because if I weren't tall, I would be fat." Immediately, I thought to myself that she must be in some kind of pain about her size. Since I did not take her statement as a slam against me, there was nothing to forgive. I realized that a heart full of unforgiveness cannot be full of love.*

The question arises, "After forgiveness, what comes next?" The answer is simple but not always easy, "More forgiving." Remember, we are not forgiving the whole person. Rather, we are forgiving individual acts of real or perceived violations. After we forgive a person for one act, we may later need to forgive them for another violation that we just remembered from long ago. When that happens, simply use the Forgiveness Process to forgive the violation.

The more we forgive, the better we get at knowing how to forgive. The more we forgive, the better we get at knowing when to forgive. Being released from the weight of unforgiveness is so great a feeling that it can become a habit. Imagine being addicted to being free from the poisonous evil of unforgiveness! That's success! Such success breeds more success. Eventually, what happened to me was that after learning to forgive and doing it enough, I developed a "quick start" form of forgiveness. That is, if I felt somehow violated, I did not take in the other person's "stuff" so there was nothing for me to forgive—nothing to take out of my heart. After I had purged enough "stuff" from my heart, I felt lighter and my spirit was lighter and my outlook on life was brighter. My face even changed. I know this because I started hearing comments such as "You sure have a beautiful smile." I simply said, "Thank you." However, I was thinking to myself, "How different from the reactions I used to get." I like the new me. I have been liberated from unforgiveness.

I like using the Forgiveness Process because it is a repeatable process that can be used for any infraction or perceived infraction. I have been able to help others get to a state of forgiveness. What a joy that is. It's good to get free myself, but it is especially rewarding to help others learn to forgive.

Forgiving becomes a habit. It is a life skill in coping with relationships. When I learned to forgive, I no longer felt like a victim because I realized that I have the power to control what I allow into my heart. Forgiving leaves me free to experience the love of people and allows me to freely give love. Others too have shared with me the results of their letting go of the past hurts and fears through forgiveness. Some of those testimonies are below. The names have been changed or obscured.

Testimony from a College Student

Ms. White,

The truth of the matter is I have gone through many hurts and disappointments: loss of loved ones, betrayal, mistreatment and misunderstanding. But after accepting God as my savior I was trying desperately to live as the Bible said I should. Yet no matter how hard I tried it seemed that people continued to hurt me, betray me, and mistreat me. So I grew tougher skin—or so I thought. I vowed not to let anyone close enough to hurt me ever again. But God made me sensitive for a reason, for the work I am commissioned to do. A closed heart is not part of my make-up. I am caring and sympathetic.

When I spoke to you and you invited me to hear your talk on "Forgiveness" it must have been orchestrated by God. You see, I had been on the Daniel fast for thirty-one days. It was day 21 when I spoke to you. And God had done so much in me, but there was still some left-over residue of some past hurts and pains. As you spoke, I was delivered, convicted and knew what I had to do. I began calling people and writing letters. I was forgiving them and asking them to forgive me. My life has drastically changed!

I can use the instruction you gave by separating people from the action that hurt me and keep that relationship. I am also a mentor to teens and have taught them the same concept. I share this with everyone that I hear speaking of themselves as victims to free them to be victors as I have become.

There is no doubt that God gave you this revelation and wisdom to heal the many hurts of the pain that resided in us for years. This healing requires action and not just prayer. I am free spiritually and my heart is open to love because you spoke the words God gave you about forgiveness. Thank you I am delivered, free to forgive and free to love. Xxxxxxx Harris

A Testimony from a Student Going Abroad

Ms. White

I just want to thank you again for the lesson on forgiveness. It was right on time, and it has changed my life tremendously. You are a wonderful lady and a great mentor. I will miss you. I am going to London to study abroad and hope to be an active member of Toastmasters when I return. Thank you again. You inspire me to mature, grow, and forgive! Because of forgiveness, I have become free.

Xxxxx Smith

A Testimony from a Church Member

Sister White,

Thank you for speaking to our Bible study class. I had never heard about forgiveness like that before. I cried when I learned that I can still forgive my sister who is deceased. I forgive her one step at a time. I want to learn more. I hope you teach more. I have so much to forgive. I am here in America because of the wars in my country. I have a lot to forgive, but I am starting with my sister and my mother. Even writing this note, I am crying tears of release. Thank you so much.

Musa Xxxxxx

A Testimony from a Coworker

Mrs. White,

When I left on Thursday, I told you that my life had changed after what you taught about forgiveness. When I went home, I told my wife about it. Thank you so much. We both thought our life as a family was over, but now we have a new chance. Thank you for your speech at Toastmasters about "How to Forgive." You are a good lady.

Xxxxx Bruce

Note: This speech mentioned above was outside a Christian setting. Forgiveness is one of those truths that God put into the universe for everyone. Anyone can benefit from forgiveness. We are to pray for and minister to all "that you may be sons of your Father in heaven; for He makes His sun rise on the evil and on the good, and sends rain on the just and on the unjust."[39]

A Testimony from a Young Friend

Miss Julia,

I remember my first reaction to your trying to teach me to forgive Frxxxxxx and Mixxxxx for breaking up our family. I said, "You want me to give them permission to walk over me? After what they did to me? I'm not wishing the best to them, so why should I forgive them? You are talking crazy! It sounds like you are on their side. When Frxxxxx walked away from me and our child, I grew to hate him and Mixxxxx."

I am so glad that you were patient with me. You gave me a little at a time. But I guess I had to hear it from other places too before I could listen to talk about forgiving those home wreckers. Remember, I called them home wreckers? Well, they are still home wreckers, but I do not have to live with that bitterness anymore. Thank you.

Regina Sawyer

Note: With permission, I have used Regina's name. When I told her I changed the names of the people whose stories are in this book, she insisted that I use her name. Her granting such permission just shows that she believes in what she is saying and desires to help others.

There is a lot to look forward to after forgiveness. Just imagine a life with less stress from unresolved family issues. This can happen through use of the Forgiveness Process. We are required to forgive. As stated early in this book, forgiveness does not necessarily imply that we should keep or allow the forgiven to stay in our lives. Forgiveness does not necessarily include restoration of the relationship. However, if the forgiven seeks reconciliation and you feel that they sincerely have changed from the past then it is incumbent upon you to listen and then decide if the relationship can be restored. Life after forgiveness is an ongoing process. The one constant that takes place after we learn to forgive is more forgiving! Do your part and trust God to do God's part.

PART 2

The Forgiveness Process

This Forgiveness Process was developed over a period of time. It is a series of steps that help a person release the things that keep them from being loving and free. The purpose of this process is to heal the memories, the patterns of physical and emotional dysfunction, and the negative belief systems that were conceived at times of disappointment, criticism, hurt, abuse, loss, rejection, humiliation, abandonment, and so on. It is to set the forgiver free to move on from the effects of these. The result of the Forgiveness Process is forgiveness. We go through the steps to bring forgiveness into our lives, and, at the same time, we release the results of unforgiveness from our being.

We have a need to forgive. We have already discussed what unforgiveness can do to us mentally, spiritually, and physically. So, we see that it is a good thing to forgive, but *how*? There are very definite steps we can take to forgive. The Forgiveness Process is listed here:

Forgiveness Process

1. **Separate the person from what they did.**
2. **Realize that the relationship is broken.**
3. **Admit your loss and allow yourself to grieve.**
4. **Try to understand the other person.**
5. **Think of individual acts of violation.**
6. **Start throwing out the junk.**
7. **Guard your heart and mind.**

We will examine each step to learn how to incorporate forgiveness into our lives. These steps do not have to be done in sequence, but it helps at first to follow the steps from top to bottom. For sake of clarity, let's call the person who did something to you the perpetrator. Let's call you the victim. The act that they did to you will be called the infraction or perpetration. The process starts.

1. Separate the person from what they did.

In your mind, separate the person from what they did to you or what you perceive they did to you. It is hard to work on forgiving the entire perpetrator all at once. Let's say that the perpetrator did several things that you did not like. You felt victimized many times by this person. Think of each of those things one by one. Try not to think of the person so much as what they did—the infractions. These infractions broke the relationship you had or potentially would have had with the perpetrator. This act falls in the category of "hate the sin, love the sinner."[40] This is a direct quote from Mahatma Gandhi, Indian political and spiritual leader (1869-1948). When we separate the person from what they did, we can go on and love the person. The scripture tells us that "If anyone says, 'I love God,' but hates a Christian brother or sister, that person is a liar; for if we don't love people we can see, how can we love God, whom we have not seen?"[41]

2. Realize that the relationship is broken.

The relationship is broken. Don't even try to pretend that it didn't bother you to be violated by the perpetrator. The violation may have been small or large. The size of the infraction doesn't even matter. Little things hurt too. Regardless of the size of the infraction, the relationship is not good. Maybe you do not want to speak to the perpetrator. Maybe it is not even safe to be around the perpetrator. Regardless, as a result of the event, you now have some extra "stuff" in your heart and mind. This "stuff" is carried around by you and this "stuff" stands in the way of your relationship with the perpetrator. It is important to note that the relation may not be fixed. It is not a necessary part of forgiveness that the relationship be restored.

3. Admit your loss and allow yourself to grieve.

As a result of this broken relationship and the resultant feelings, you have suffered a loss. Allow yourself to grieve over this loss. Grief happens in stages like: shock, intense grief, and readjustment.[42] Later, we will look at some examples of some losses and how people dealt with them. Sometimes people are actually afraid to face their loss or their pain. It's sometimes easier to go into denial with statements such as "No, it didn't hurt me. I was just mad." Aha! Loss of happiness. A robbery leaves us feeling violated in many ways - loss of innocence. Allow yourself to grieve—to really feel the depth of your loss. With that loss came pain, hatred of self, hatred of others, bitterness, resentment, anger, fear, and other destructive emotions.

4. Try to understand the other person.

This is a very important step because it gets us out of ourselves and broadens our thinking. It can be very hard because of the fear that if I understood the perpetrator, I might "let down my guard" and empathize with them. It may be too late to mend the relationship, but not too late to understand the other person. Then you are ready to tackle step 5 of the Forgiveness Process.

5. Think of individual acts of violation.

There probably are many acts or events where one perceives that the perpetrator did them wrong. Pick some. Pick ones where the pain has been rehearsed over and over again. These are the ones that are doing the most damage to you emotionally, physically, and spiritually. In this step of the Forgiveness Process comes the realization that you don't love nor hate the entire person all at once. Think of the individual acts of violation and start to throw out the hurtful residue of those violations—real or perceived.

6. Start throwing out the junk.

If you can throw out the junk that has accumulated in your heart, you will be free! Throwing out the junk is the actual act of forgiveness. Out of forgiveness comes healing. For each act or event, think about just that act—not about the person whom you perceived did you wrong. As you think about the acts or violations, many times the same feelings that you experienced at the time of the violation will come back to you. It is just as if you are back there again. You are still tied to the weight of that ugly feeling. The weight ties you down as surely as if there were an anchor pulling you under water. One by one, event by event, think of how each violation made you feel and decide that you do not want to feel that way anymore. One good thing to do at this point is to pray and ask God to remove the pain, the anxiety, depression, insecurity, and other residue from those happenings. No longer keep a running inventory of those negative things! Cry, if you feel like it, but let go of each thing. Those are the healing type of tears. These purges will not take place all at once. Over the years, as you think of other events, stop and forgive.

7. Guard your heart and mind.

For the rest of your life, there will be events that will happen not to your choosing. People may say or do things that you think are aimed at hurting you. Here is where you stop and remember that: Whatever comes your way, the choice to let in hurt, bitterness, pain, or resentment is up to you. Choose to guard both your heart and your mind. It's a process to get rid of unforgiveness! You can do this. Remember the steps in the Forgiveness Process and apply these steps immediately. As you learn to apply these steps quickly, you don't allow stressful stuff to permeate your mind, your body, your spirit! There is an old saying that "An ounce of prevention is worth a pound of cure." Likewise, it is better to guard your being from unforgiveness because the prevention of unforgiveness is much easier thing than going for the cure.

The Forgiveness Process

1. **Separate the person from what they did.**
2. **Realize that the relationship is broken.**
3. **Admit your loss and allow yourself to grieve.**
4. **Try to understand the other person.**
5. **Think of individual acts of violation.**
6. **Start throwing out the junk.**
7. **Guard your heart and mind.**

Although the forgiveness process seems simple to learn and to do, it is not always easy. It is hard work. It requires that you stick with it.

Be persistent. Eventually, it will become easier. The freedom brought about by using the process is such a joyful thing that you will want to use the Forgiveness Process rather than take "junk" into your heart. As step 7 becomes a habit, you will realize that you have a skill that keeps you from taking in "stuff" that you need to forgive. Forgiving is a life skill that means freedom and joy, and love are yours.

PART 3

Stories of Forgiving

These "Stories of Forgiving" are all true stories. Most were told to the author. Some stories were gleaned from news media or movies. For each person relating their story directly, the author acted as the Forgiveness Coach if they chose to go through the steps of the Forgiveness Process.

Ramona's Story

Ramona has physical beauty and the personality of one who suffers post-traumatic stress disorder. She went through a lot. Ramona was an angry child who grew into an angry young woman. Her teenage father walked away from her mother and two older brothers. A little while later, she was also abandoned by her teenage mother who dropped the children off at Ramona's grandparents' house and never came back to get them. She did visit on rare occasions. These visits only served to raise Ramona's hopes and then dash those hopes to bits when her mother left again. Ramona cried and begged to go with her mother but was left behind each time. Many times, Ramona ran after the car, crying and screaming for her mother to stop the car—and stop the pain.

Day after day, Ramona waited for her mother to come back. Day after day, she ached with pain for her tremendous loss. The days turned into weeks. The weeks turned into months. The months turned into years. As time progressed, Ramona's feelings also progressed. She went from experiencing pain and longing to bitterness and resentment. She endured a lot of loneliness even though there were other people around. In fact, several cousins also lived with Ramona's grandparents. Ramona felt that the other cousins were favored and that she and her brothers were blamed and abused for things they did not do. As if the verbal and physical abuse by the frazzled grandparents was not enough, Ramona was also raped. Ramona was raped by her father's best friend when she was only seven years old. He threatened to kill her if she told. She kept quiet. She was a scared and hurt little girl.

At school, Ramona became withdrawn at times and very aggressive at other times. She thought she was a "bad girl" and that is how she acted. Later, Ramona was raped by an uncle. The day after this rape, Ramona's teacher noticed that Ramona was hurt and talked with Ramona after class. This time Ramona told her teacher who followed up with Children's Services and the grandparents. The grandmother told the social worker that Ramona was accustomed to telling lies and that this must be one of those times. An outraged, scared, and very embarrassed grandmother became even more abusive to Ramona. After everyone had left, the grandmother "spanked" Ramona and called her a liar. The grandmother said that she did not believe Ramona and forced Ramona to apologize to her rapist. The grandmother never did tell Ramona's mother and dared Ramona to tell her mother.

When I met Ramona, she was loud, crude, and did not seem to care if she hurt others. I was reminded of something someone had told me once: "Hurting people hurt people." After several months of talking with Ramona, she told me that I was the only person she trusted. I believed that she trusted no one. I asked her if she wanted to stop the pain. I told her that life had thrown her some nasty curves, but that I thought she could stop the pain through forgiveness. After several conversations about forgiveness, I asked Ramona if she were ready to try forgiving those who had hurt her. Almost to my shock, she agreed to try!

We went through the Forgiveness Process in detail. We talked in detail as I explained each step to her. Then I asked Ramona to write down as many incidents that caused pain as she could think of. Each incident was put on a separate piece of orange paper. I assured her that she did not deserve to be abandoned by her parents. It was not her fault that her grandparents were abusive. There was nothing that she did to cause the rapists to attack her. She had grown up in a difficult situation. We talked about several things, but I asked her not to show me any of the things that she wrote about. I did not want her to be embarrassed or to ever think that I would betray her trust. One by one, we went through her lists and prayed that God would stop the pain associated with that incident. Ramona resolved to let go of the "stuff" that had been weighing her down. There were many people and many incidents to forgive, but we decided to concentrate on forgiving her mother. We followed the Forgiveness Process. We looked at each step and did not leave that step until we were comfortable with each step. It is so hard to admit that a parent—especially one's mother—has been one who has hurt us. It seems to be a natural tendency to defend the parent and go on hurting. I felt that if Ramona could forgive her mother, then it would be easier to work on forgiving the other perpetrators.

The Forgiveness Process

1. Separate the person from what they did.
2. Realize that the relationship is broken.
3. Admit your loss and allow yourself to grieve.
4. Try to understand the other person.
5. Think of individual acts of violation.
6. Start throwing out the junk.
7. Guard your heart and mind.

Ramona's Exercise in Forgiving

Following the steps of the Forgiveness Process, Ramona started on her journey of forgiveness. At first, it was hard because Ramona held so much hatred for her mother who left her and did not protect her from all the abuse Ramona suffered. Eventually, we started. As Ramona's Forgiveness Coach, I led her through the steps.

1 Separate the person from what they did.

We discussed Ramona's mother and the need to separate her from the act of the abandonment. Her mother was a person who did something wrong. This allowed Ramona to see her mother separately from being the deserter. I assured Ramona that she was not to blame for her mother's actions. I coached Ramona to not look for blame, but to just name what had happened. Name it, don't blame it. Hate what she did, but do not hate your mother. Ramona caught on to this concept. To Ramona, now it was all right to love her mother and yet hate what she did to Ramona and her brothers.

2 Realize that the relationship is broken.

Ramona kept saying that she hated her mother. Looking at Ramona's twisted face, it was easy to believe that she was living with hatred and bitterness for her mother and everyone else. We talked more until Ramona agreed that the relation between parent and child had been broken. Ramona did not even call her "Mother" or "Mom" but called her mother by her first name. We discussed the fact that the relationship may or may not be mended. Regardless, Ramona realized that the relationship was broken. This caused a lot of grief for the loss. Ramona cried hard.

3 Admit your loss and allow yourself to grieve.

Ramona had been holding onto the notion that her mother would act like a mother and reunite her family into a tight family unit. This was not to happen. Ramona cried. She cried for herself and she cried for her deep pain. She cried in shoulder-heaving pain. When Ramona took the next step, she cried for her mother.

4 Try to understand the other person.

This step was especially hard because Ramona did not want to try to understand her mother. Ramona said, "I don't want to try to understand her because it is easy to understand that she hurt me when she went off and left me." Soon, we started talking about Ramona's mother—how she had been just a child when she had Ramona. Ramona's father had vanished leaving Ramona's mother alone with three children. Ramona was the youngest. Left alone, Ramona's mother must have been bewildered. How would she make it? She thought her children would be better off with their grandparents. So she dropped the children off and went to live in another city where she got a job. Ramona seemed overwhelmed by the enormity of her feelings, so I explained that it may be better to think of a little at a time. It is almost impossible to forgive the whole person. It is much easier to think of individual acts that the person did.

5 Think of individual acts of violation.

Ramona remembered several things that hurt her during her childhood. For example, Ramona wished that her mother would rescue her from the abuse perpetrated by her grandparents. On those seldom occasions when her mother visited, Ramona recalled the hurt of being left behind each time. Ramona recalled broken promises. Although Ramona hated the rapists, she blamed her mother for leaving her where she could be raped. The list grew long and I encouraged Ramona to write each act on a separate piece of paper so that it would be easier to start throwing out the junk one incident at a time. Later, when other incidents are thought of, the same steps could be done.

6 Start throwing out the junk

In this step, I had Ramona look at each piece of paper. Each sheet of paper contained a different incident or act of perpetration. I did not ask her to share the contents of the paper with me, but I did want her to share her feelings. I asked Ramona how she felt at the time of the incident and how she felt now. Often, the old feelings were relived. Ramona cried when she talked about how she felt and said she still felt the pain. I asked her if she was ready to let go of those feelings. When she indicated that she was ready to let go, we prayed about each incident. One-by-one, the incidents were examined. Each time, we asked God to take away the pain associated with that incident. As each incident was forgiven, that piece of paper was destroyed. Ramona was throwing the junk out of her heart. This did not mean that Ramona forgot any incident, but she did forget the pain and was ready for the next step in the Forgiveness Process.

7 Guard your heart and mind.

Once the heart and mind are made clear of the pain of unforgiveness, it is important to not let in more "stuff." When a would-be-perpetrator brings an unwanted incident into your presence, simply know that that "stuff" is not yours. Don't accept it into your heart. Leave it with the person who brought it to you. It is their issue. That "stuff" belongs to them. This is like forgiving ahead of time. It is like having a shield around your heart and mind.

After going through the "Forgiveness Process" for Ramona's mother, we worked through incidents perpetrated by other persons in Ramona's life. We worked through the process for Ramona's father's deserting the family. Next came each rapist. We looked at teachers who did not understand this angry little girl. Then we looked at the grandparents, especially the grandmother. Ramona understood that the broken relationships did not need to be mended in order to forgive. In some cases, however, Ramona wanted that restoration to take place. In other cases, she wanted the perpetrator to know that she forgave them in order to bring a sense of closure and to take back the power that she had lost to her perpetrators. Ramona and her mother mended their relationship and became close. They were so close in age that they also became friends before her mother died of cancer.

Jeannie's Story

Jeannie and Valerie Lee Barnett were buddies in the eighth grade. They had several classes together except the last period of the day. Even then, Jeannie and Valerie Lee met after school to say, "Bye" to each other. They talked about everything—school, family, music, and movies. Valerie Lee told Jeannie that her younger sister could yodel just like the people in the Swiss Alps. Jeannie wanted to hear it. One day, Valerie Lee had her sister Vickie meet them after school so that Jeannie could hear Vickie yodel. Valerie Lee had bragged about Vickie so much that the appointed meeting was a joyful occasion. Valerie Lee and Jeannie waited a few minutes and Vickie showed up. She put down her books and drew a deep breath. She began to yodel. This unusual performance was very fascinating to Jeannie. Jeannie thanked her friends, and they turned their separate ways for home.

The following week was a big semester test for the eighth graders. Jeannie was the top performer in Ms. Trinstead's U.S. History class. Ms. Trinstead had even taken the time to explain why Jeannie was the top performer in her class. Ms. Trinstead said, "Jeannie always had her assignments completed and turned in on time. Her work is very neat and well organized. Jeannie follows instructions. She reads assignments and outside sources so that she always has something interesting to add or a thought-provoking question to ask. That's why Jeannie is the top student."

Valerie Lee asked Jeannie to study with her for the big semester test. Jeannie agreed and invited a quiet girl named Katie to study with Valerie Lee and her. Trying to decide where to gather for the study session, first Jeannie suggested Katie's house. This was ruled out because Katie's mother worked and gave strict orders not to have other children come over in her absence. Next, Jeannie's house was ruled out because there was just no space to study. Jeannie usually did her homework on the kitchen table after the dinner dishes were cleared. Sometimes she used the desk in the living room if no one else had grabbed it first. Besides, there were so many siblings. Always, the younger siblings were running about the house, looking at television, practicing piano lessons, or getting homework help from the older siblings. Mother was busy getting dinner ready before Jeannie's father came home from work. The family always ate together. That house was just too busy. It was ruled out.

Next, Jeannie asked Valerie Lee if they could all study at Valerie Lee's house. It was bound to be roomy and quiet since the family was so small. Valerie Lee declined. When ask why she had declined, Valerie Lee hung her head and said, "My mother said that no coloreds are allowed in our house." Valerie Lee was embarrassed to tell her friends this. Jeannie and Katie were just plain old hurt.

Jeannie said she felt demeaned, belittled, betrayed, and devastated. She was deeply hurt and offended by what happened. Although the offense itself was quite serious and painful, what hurt most of all was that a friend had done it. The feeling of betrayal was intense. Never in life had Jeannie encountered such blatant racism face-to-face. What a rude awakening. Jeannie was completely taken off guard by the rejection. In her innocence, Jeannie thought hers and Valerie Lee's relationship was rock solid. The relationship was broken! Never again would Jeannie and Valerie Lee be good friends. Once they left junior high school, they never saw each other again.

Jeannie's Journey to Forgiveness

"My forgiveness of Valerie Lee took place over the years. Even before I knew the importance of forgiveness, I knew that I did not want to live with that pain. I would 'forget' about it for a while and eventually go back to where I was—hurting. Whenever I told anyone about it, I started to cry. In high school, I felt shielded from racism because most of the students were the same race as I. I found an old tape playing in my head where I heard my dad say, 'Treat them nice, but keep on going. Don't trust white folk as far as you can throw them.' Mother said to take each person on their own merit. I must admit, however, I felt like Mother's advice had let me in for hurt. I felt like I should have listened more to Dad.

"Years later, I realized that deep down I was still hurting and feeling so much like I was thought of as a 'colored' second class citizen or less by Valerie Lee and her family. Finally, while preparing a speech for Toastmasters Club at where I was a member, I realized that I would have to forgive Valerie Lee in order to feel better about myself and the members of the group that I was managing. I couldn't afford not to trust them. I was managing a high visibility, company-wide conversion project. The project would last over three years, and we converted computer systems from branches all over the United States and some parts of Canada. Our success as a group depended on that trust. It didn't matter what their racial backgrounds were, we had a job to do, and I must not give anyone the same power that I had given to Valerie Lee.

"I had been introduced to the Forgiveness Process by the Forgiveness Coach. I used that process to the best of my ability without the help of the coach. I was feeling like I was on the road to leaving the past hurt permanently behind me. In that speech, I told of the example of the POW held in Japanese captivity during World War II. He was treated brutally but decided not to live with those haunting memories again. He forgave his torturer. As I gave that speech, others also seemed to get great relief—a new lease on life. One person, a big, burly Lumber Department manager, said with tears in his eyes that my speech on forgiveness meant a new outlook for him. He said, 'This speech transformed me.'

"I did not go through the entire Forgiveness Process in that speech because the speech was a timed ten-minute speech. I had applied the Forgiveness Process to the pain and suffering from the Valerie Lee event. Here's what I did:

1 Separate the person from what they did.

Valerie Lee was Valerie Lee, and the things she did were acts. In so thinking, I had separated Valerie Lee from the thing she said that hurt me so badly. I could now cherish the memories of our laughing together every day. I could love Valerie Lee regardless what she did. I did not have to like what she did in order to love her. What a revelation! Now I was not divided in my feelings. I was free to love Valerie Lee completely, but I hated what happened between us. We never shared secrets or laughed at silly little incidents again. Now I could see the relationship for what it was—broken! I was ready for step 2 in the Forgiveness Process.

2 Realize that the relationship is broken.

It was painful to realize that the relationship was not what I would have liked. I wanted to feel that the friendship had been reciprocal between me and Valerie Lee. As result of what happened, I felt disrespected by Valerie Lee. We weren't friends. Our relationship did not make me feel good. I realize now that I was so angry about being 'colored' because it was a source of exclusion, pain, fear, and suspicion. The relationship was broken. I faced this painful realization and was ready for step 3 in the Forgiveness Process.

3 Admit your loss and allow yourself to grieve.

Once I came to grips with the fact that I couldn't do anything to control the other person, I grieved. I let it go. Then I would remember some other aspect that I had forgotten and have to go through the loss all over again. In my mind, I had to continually separate the person from the act. I had to keep going back to step 1 and step 2 before I could go through step 3 as often as I needed. Now that Valerie Lee was a separate entity from the acts she did, nothing else could break the relationship because it was already broken. No more shock. No more pain from the relationship being broken. Now I knew that my pain was coming from what I had taken away from the event or the act. I had a choice. No longer helpless, I was ready to move on to the step 4 in the Forgiveness Process.

4 Try to understand the other person.

This is a very important step because I have to think of Valerie Lee, not myself. Here, I would try to understand Valerie Lee. It was so hard because there were times when I must have been afraid that if I understood her, I might 'let down my guard' and empathize with her. It was too late to mend our relationship, but not too late to understand her. I thought about that day in junior high school. I remembered the pained look on Valerie Lee's face. She was only following her mom's orders. Valerie Lee and I had been so close that I came to realize that she was as hurt as I was. I was now ready to tackle step 5 of the Forgiveness Process.

5 Think of individual acts of violation.

In step 5 of the Forgiveness Process, I realized that there was only that one incidence between Valerie Lee and me that was so hurtful. I thought that I really ought to be trying to forgive her mother for trying to instill such racism. But that's another case for some other time. I was ready to move on to step 6 of the Forgiveness Process.

6 Start throwing out the junk.

Forgiveness brings about healing. For each act or event, I thought about just that act—not about Valerie Lee. As I thought about that day, the same feelings that I cried about then came back to me. It was just as if I were back there again. I prayed and asked God to remove the pain and the feelings of self-loathing that came with being 'colored' back then. No, my race has not changed, but my self-worth sure has! I am ready to take the next step in the Forgiving Process.

7 Guard your heart and mind.

The Forgiveness Coach had told me that forgiveness is a choice. She said that when we forgive, we collect all our power to decide what and who we want to let into our hearts. I like having love in my heart. I will guard my heart. When anything comes my way that I do not want to take in, I will start right then to apply the Forgiveness Process. To the best of my ability, I will try to see the other person as just that—the other person. Whatever negative things or hurts they bring to me, I will not accept into my heart. In addition, I will forgive them right away! I'm free and I want to stay that way."

Stella's Story

This is Stella's story—told in Stella's own words:

"There was no one to say, 'I'm sorry that happened to you.' My mother was abusive to me. As far back as I could remember, I felt that she didn't love me. I was the second child in a family of eight children. I was told many times that the pregnancy that bore me was an unwanted pregnancy, and that the baby was unwanted. Never were these stories followed up with a statement such as 'But you were a cute little baby and I loved you.' To the contrast, my dad often made such positive remarks, and I guess that helped me a lot. I learned a little song in Sunday school. The song went like this:

Jesus loves the little children.
All the children of the world.
Red and Yellow,
Black and White.
They are precious in His sight.
Jesus loves the little children of the world.

"The message in that song was my saving grace. I was so happy to know that Jesus loved me, but I wanted my mother to love me, also. Too often, however, I heard my mother relay some ugly stories about me and I took them in. The rejection never let up. She told ugly stories to me about how evil I was as a baby. She told these stories to her family. When a neighbor commented that I was a sweet little girl, my mother said, 'Oh, not Stella. Stella is bad. Susie is the sweet one.' Susie was even allowed to sit on Mother's lap."

Stella said, "I was a year older than Susie, yet I had to always move over so that Susie could be held. When I was brushed aside with such words as, 'Move now so that I can hold the baby,' I was crushed. I wanted a hug too—sometimes, just sometimes. As I got older, the statements became harsher. There was even physical abuse in the form of shouting and hitting. I began to think of myself as bad and ugly. I did not have many friends.

"I thought about committing suicide, but I didn't really want to die. I just wanted my mother to love me and not hate me. Worse, I did not want to hate myself so much. I went through the family album and scratched out the face of every picture of me.

"Things got pretty bad during my high school years. When my baby sister was born, Mother and I quit speaking at all. For almost two months, I suffered with laryngitis and could not speak. No one noticed. One of my high school teachers, my mentor, visited my home and brought it to the attention of my mother. My mentor's interest in me was refreshing. She saw me as a very bright student and gave me many opportunities to participate in local, state, and regional academic competitive events. The extra care and attention meant the world to me. I graduated at the top of my class and went on to college.

"Later I got married and we started our own family. Determined to make each of my children know that they were loved, I spent time with each individual. Sometimes when they all wanted to be held at the same time, I got down on the floor where we could all huddle and cuddle. Before I could love my husband and our children, however, I had to learn to love myself. Loving myself was hard work because I realized that I had to forgive Mother for the love I did not get from her."

Stella's Journey to Forgiveness

"My recovery through forgiveness took place in stages. I would start with one stage, go to another, and go back where I was—hurting. I thought I could forgive my mother in one big session. I thought if I just tried hard enough, I could forgive everything. But the pain kept coming back. It was after we had children that I really wanted to have a better relationship with the grandmother of our children.

"There was no one to share the pain. My husband couldn't help much because little did I know it, but he had his own pain to deal with. Besides, I didn't want to tell him too much negative because I didn't want him to hate my mother. I also didn't want him and others to feel that I was a complainer. When I did try to talk with those closest to me in my family, they made hurtful statements such as 'Just try to forget it.' Well, it wouldn't go away. Finally, I realized without knowing the process of forgiveness that I would have to forgive my mother in order to feel better about myself.

"I learned through self-help books and classes that I was *Born to Win*, that *I'm OK and You're OK*. I learned that God does not create junk.

I even learned that I am a beautiful woman and could look at myself in a public bathroom mirror just like the other women. I learned that God had created me for a specific purpose. I reasoned that if all this was true, then I must be somebody. I started casting out the negative tapes that played in my head. I replaced them with positive statements which I didn't even believe yet, but I came to know through reading the Book of Proverbs from the Bible that 'The tongue has the power of life and death, and those who love it will eat its fruit.' I started powerful confessions with my tongue. Eventually, I came to believe more and more that I was a wonderful person. Mother was wrong. I didn't feel good leaving Mother at such a negative place in my life, so I started working through our relationship—alone. I learned that I had to forgive her. I thought I could do it through intellect and understanding that forgiveness was necessary. I found that I didn't know *how* to forgive.

"To forgive Mother, I went through certain stages and steps. It took a long time—years—because I was going through stages and steps, but I was feeling my way. I did not have a guide on *how* to forgive. I found myself denying that there was anything wrong with our relationship. Yet I was afraid that the pain would keep coming back. I did not even understand how anyone really loved doing things with their mother. I felt sad, angry, bitter, distrustful, resentful, and oh so deeply hurt. I longed for the love that others seemed to have from their mothers. I seldom smiled. Lots of times, I had a frown on my face. This further distanced me from others. I was in a shell of protection from expecting love and not getting love. I felt neglected and rejected. How can one feel this way? It just happens that we can't control our feelings—only what we do with our feelings. I decided to face my feelings. I grieved about not having that close relationship. I had just taken step 3 in the Forgiveness Process. I didn't realize it, but I had been working on this step for years!

"After Mother died at an early age, I grieved even more for the loss of my mother, my children's grandmother, and the chance to heal our relationship. I started to use the Forgiveness Process in my mind. I was feeling like I was on the road to recovery. As I shared it with others, they also seemed to get great relief—a new lease on life. I went through the steps:

1. Separate the person from what they did.

Mother was mother, and the things she did were things she did— some I liked and some I did not like. I could love Mother regardless what she did. I did not have to like everything she did in order to love her. What a revelation! Now I was not divided in my feelings. I was free to love Mother completely, but I hated some of the things she did or that I thought she did against me. Now I could see the relationship for what it was—broken! I was ready for step 2 in the Forgiveness Process.

2. Realize that the relationship is broken.

It was painful to realize that the relationship was not what I would have liked. I wanted to feel supported in love. I wanted to feel that my mother would affirm me to others and myself. Most of the time, I felt disrespected by her. We weren't friends. Our relationship did not make me feel good. Did she feel the same way? I don't know, but it felt bad all the time. I tried being 'the good child' so that she would like me. I followed her around and listened to her talk about old times. I ate the things she liked, including squash. It didn't seem to work. The relationship was broken. I faced this painful realization and was ready for step 3 in the Forgiveness Process.

3. Admit your loss and allow yourself to grieve.

I already had good practice in this step. For decades, I had gone through life feeling that love and respect were missing. I longed for them, but came to grips with the fact that I didn't feel it was there and that I couldn't do anything to control the other person—my mother. I grieved. I let it go. Then I would remember some other event that I had forgotten and have to go through the loss all over again. I realized that I had not yet separated the person from the act. Once I did step 1 and step 2, I could go through step 3 as often as I needed because now mother was separate from the acts, and nothing else could break the relationship because it was already broken. No more shock. No more pain from the relationship being broken. Now I knew that my pain was coming from what I had taken away from the event or the act. I had a choice. No longer helpless, I was ready to move on to step 4 in the Forgiveness Process.

4. Try to understand the other person.

Step 4 is a very important step, but it was a hard step. My job in this step is to try to understand Mother. It was so hard because there were times when I wanted to hate her for what I perceived she had done to me. Neighbors always referred to her as 'sweet,' but I did not feel her sweetness. It was a few months after she died that I began to understand her. After she died, we found her journal in which she told her life story. Her life was not filled with love. Her parents seemed like typical parents in many ways, but Mother's story told of being not favored by her mother and treated very sternly by her father.

Mother's father was a crusty entrepreneur who struggled to be a successful farmer, a contractor who built barns and farm houses—mostly from lumber from his small sawmill. At one point, he was the town blacksmith. A mulatto, he did not trust white people or black people. Through good budgeting, some frugality, building good financial partnerships with his bankers, and the hard work of the entire family, Mother's father was a pillar in the community. He built the local church from his resources and dictated whose name went on each of the stained-glass windows in that church. Mother told us of his harshness. He was partial to Mother's older sister and one other of the girls.

Mother's mother was partial to two of the children too. Neither of them was my mother. She told of being hurt by the seeming injustices caused by this partiality. My heart went out to her. No wonder she treated me the way she did—it was done to her! Because of Mother's journal, I now understood more about her. When I understood her, I guess I didn't take it so personally anymore. It was too late to mend our relationship, but not too late to understand her. I was now ready to tackle the next step in the Forgiveness Process.

5. Think of individual acts of violation.

There were many acts or events where I perceived that Mother did me wrong. I picked some. It wasn't hard because I had rehearsed the pain over a lifetime. In fact, I pushed aside many of the good things she did for me. She taught me family loyalty to my siblings and my parents. She taught me to respect authority—to always pay attention in school and church. Though she could not sing, she taught us to love music through songbooks and piano lessons throughout our childhood. Mother taught me to sew. She was a meticulous seamstress who made all our clothes and sewed shirts for a famous men's shirt company. She taught me to think and never to be defeated by circumstances. I can still hear her say something like 'Well, let's try this. There is more than one way to skin a cat.'

"Mother was always there to defend us as a group. She nursed us when we were sick. She taught us to pray and took us to choir practice, Sunday school, and church. Of course, most of the things were joint efforts of my mother and my dad. But right now, I'm talking about Mother. Daddy built us a playhouse and jungle gym in the back yard. Mother kept a watchful eye on us and even taught us to use our imaginations to play games. She even taught us to make beautiful mud pies and to decorate our mud cakes using a mixture of lime, water, and food coloring. We had unlimited and safe fun playing together! I'm grateful for all those things and more, but I also remembered the hurts. In step 5 of the Forgiveness Process, I realized that I couldn't love nor hate the entire person all at once. I would have to think of the individual acts of violation and start to overcome the hurtful residue of those violations—real or perceived. I was ready to move on to step 6 of the Forgiveness Process.

6. Start throwing out the junk.

If I could throw out the junk that had accumulated in my heart, I would be free! Throwing out the junk is the actual act of forgiveness.

Out of forgiveness comes healing. For each act or event, I thought about just that act—not about Mother. As I thought about them, most of the same feelings that I cried about as a child came back to me. It was just as if I were back there again. I was still tied to the weight of that ugly feeling. The weight was tied to me as surely as if there were an anchor pulling me under. Yes, those feelings had not left me. They were just stuffed away, quietly robbing me of self-esteem, happiness, self-worth, and other positive energy. The bitterness and the resentment were toxic to me. One by one, event by event, I thought of how each made me feel and decided that I didn't want to feel that way anymore. I prayed and asked God to remove the pain, the anxiety, depression, and insecurity resulting from those happenings. I did not want to keep inventory of those negative things! I cried as I let go of those things. I'm sure they were the healing type of tears. I cried as I allowed God to fill me with love for Mother. In the process, I also got more love for myself. These purges did not take place all at once. In the coming years, as I think of other events, I will stop and forgive. Now I am ready for the important step 7 in the Forgiving Process.

7.Guard your heart and mind.

The Forgiveness Coach said, "For the rest of your life, there will be events that will happen not to your choosing. People may say or do things that you think are aimed at hurting you. Here is where you stop and remember that whatever comes your way, the choice to let in hurt, bitterness, pain, or resentment is up to you. Make a conscious choice to guard your heart and your mind. It's definitely a process to get rid of unforgiveness! You can do this! You must remember the steps in the Forgiveness Process and apply these steps immediately. As you learn to apply these steps quickly, you don't allow stressful stuff to permeate your mind, your body, your spirit! There is an old saying that 'An ounce of prevention is worth a pound of cure.' Better to guard your being from unforgiveness because the prevention of unforgiveness is much easier thing than going for the cure. Hurray! You can forgive and will carry this skill throughout your life. You can also teach others to get free."

Chandler's Story

"My father was a mean man. Nothing was ever right to him. Easily provoked, he abused my mother in many ways. Not only did he beat her on a regular basis, he also verbally abused her in front of her children or anybody else who happened to be present. Often, I would awaken to the muffled cries of my mother's pain. I heard the sound of his fist meeting her flesh. It was that 'thud' sound as Mom's body had ended the journey of my dad's pugilistic thrust. The slaps were like firecrackers bursting against an undeserving target.

I knew that the next morning I would see fresh bruises and a tired, stressed mother who appeared so small and helpless. I wanted so badly to rush to her side and take her away from the situation. But I was just a little boy—too small to confront my dad. It was awful. My sisters were afraid too. Everyone was afraid of my dad's wrath. I hated my dad. I dreamed of the day when I would retaliate. I also hated my mother for taking the abuse. I felt guilty because I could not prevent the next attack no matter how good my behavior.

"One morning, as I was dressing for school and trying to comfort my mother at the same time, I asked her, 'Mom, why don't you just leave him?' I just wanted to survive and I wanted my mother to survive. She said, 'One day you will understand why I don't just leave. Your dad makes the money in the family.'

Now I am a grown man and I still don't understand. I actually remember thinking to myself, 'What family?' As far as I was concerned, we didn't have a family. We had a living arrangement with a Kodiak bear in the Alpha Male position and several cubs who cowered to a level so low that we almost forgot our own identities. Our main concern every day was how we could please the Kodiak bear or become so invisible that he wouldn't see us. I was not only angry; I had total hatred for my father.

"I have two sisters. One of them hates men so much that she chose to never have a woman-to-man relationship. I think she was afraid that she would suffer the same fate as our mother. She is a lesbian. She seeks to be loved by women—the only source of love in her formative years. My younger sister suffers from severe depression. I guess her anger got the best of her. Lately, I have been talking to them about forgiveness. They don't want to hear it. I know that forgiveness is the answer to my healing, but I just can't seem to forgive my father. I think, 'How can one man be so mean?' Then I know the answer: he was treated meanly by his father. He was beaten about the least 'infraction' and punished in cruel ways. It's no wonder he is so mean. So, I reluctantly start to understand my father. I'm not ready to forgive him.

"I am looking for ways to stop my pain, my hatred, my bitterness, my loathing. I don't want to continue to live with this toxic way of thinking. This 'stuff' colors all my relationships. I can remember feeling helpless and unloved. I also remember the time that I stood up to my father when he was about to hurt my mother. I'll never forget that. I stood up for my mother. Actually, I was also angry with my mother for years. It was not until I began to see her as a small helpless creature that I lost some of my anger with her. I hated the fact that she did not take us away from my father's abuse. I'll work on forgiving them both, but I am not ready yet. Thank you for your help. I have a lot of work to do."

Note: As Forgiveness Coach, I wanted to help Chandler forgive his parents and be free of the anger, pain, bitterness, resentment, and self-torture. Those hateful thoughts that had become Chandler's childhood memories were like poison to his life – mind, body, and spirit! Chandler could be free. However, Chandler had rehearsed the hurt, bitterness, pain, and anger for so long that it was a habit, a destructive habit. Habits are hard to break and can be like an addiction that brings death. There is a verse (1 John 3:14) that reads, "We know that we have passed from death unto life, because we love the brethren. He that loveth not his brethren abides in death." The torture of unforgiveness was too hard for Chandler to turn loose the hateful thoughts toward his father. Rehearsing those thoughts and thinking what he wished he could have done to help his mother made Chandler feel guilty. All those unhealthy thoughts! Chandler was not ready to move on. I referred him to a professional therapist.

Allen's Story

"My father left us at an early age. Have I forgiven him or dismissed him? He's dead now. It's not like I have any animosity against him. There is emptiness where I wonder what he looked like, how he turned out. Do I have brothers and sisters out there? I had a wonderful stepfather. I must admit that I haven't spent a lot of time thinking about my birth father. Childhood memories include his fighting with my mother. I was small, but I wanted to protect my mother from his cruelty. I was four or five years old when he left. I was glad when he left so that my mother would not get hurt by him. I don't remember liking my father.

"One time, I mentioned that maybe I would try to find my birth father. My aunt Colleen advised me to not look for him. She said, 'You are healthy, and you love your stepfather very much.' Although I can't remember my birth father very much, I don't have anything to forgive. I don't feel any bitterness or resentment toward him. Maybe I lived a better life without him. I don't wish anything but good for him. I hope he had a good life."

Charley Mae's Story

This is Charley Mae's story of hazing in the sorority to which she pledged. Charley Mae says that she had always wanted to be in the same sorority as her mother. Charley Mae remembered accompanying her mother to various sorority functions and committee meetings. Often, the committees met in her house. There was always so much camaraderie. The women in the sorority showed a lot of passion for what they were doing—usually some project to benefit those less fortunate or some project to increase awareness on certain issues, or to add to the enjoyment of the cultural environment in our city. One of the most convincing things to make Charley Mae know that she wanted to be in this sorority was the way the members treated each other. Most of the time, the sorors were polite and respectful to each other. Even when they disagreed, they would address each other as "My sister" in warm tones.

Charley Mae recounted, "One day, while shopping with Mother, a strange woman approached her. She had seen the sweater that Mother was wearing and noted that they belonged to the same sorority. There were squeals of delight at meeting each other. They acted as though they had found a long-lost family member. Instantly, each woman greeted the other with the sorority handshake. They talked briefly about the colleges they had attended and told the names of the chapters and the years they 'went over' into the sorority. I was impressed. I asked Mother, 'Who was that lady?' Mother told me that she was in the same sorority and that whenever she met a sorority sister anywhere in the world, there was a special sisterly love that was shared between them. I certainly liked the sound of that. After all, I didn't have a sister.

"As the years rolled by, my desire to be in the same sorority as my mother grew stronger. I entered college and eventually pledged into that sorority. What a shocker! The Big Sisters acted like they did not like us at all. We were kept from sleeping. We were commanded to run errands for the Big Sisters at all hours of the day or night. It felt more like we were being initiated into a gang rather than into a sorority! Where was the sisterhood? Even my fellow pledgees, my 'line sisters,' were in constant disagreement. We had signed a pledge that we would not succumb to the hazing that had been a negative part of the history for so many Greek letter organizations—sororities and fraternities. Yet here we were being hazed unmercifully. I told my mother about it, and she advised me to get my line sisters to stand together in keeping our pledge to not be hazed.

"Mother caught an early morning flight and came to our college campus and talked with the pledges and her young campus sorors. She called the chapter advisor and the regional director. The chapter advisor was not aware of the secret meetings and unmerciful hazing. The regional director turned a deaf ear to the complaints and allowed the hazing to continue.

"My mother said to the pledges, 'You are not in college to flunk out. Don't waste your parents' money like that. Do your homework! Learn the sorority history, songs, and other information. But do not allow yourselves to be hazed.' All agreed at first. Then they got scared and allowed themselves to be hazed—all except me.

"As a result of my stance, I was ostracized by my line sisters and berated by the Big Sisters. I was totally miserable. Fortunately, my mother was very supportive. She told me that I was as good as already in the sorority because I had gone through enough, had already paid my money, had the grade-point average needed, and turned in all the forms and requirements to the Sorority National Headquarters. When the pledge period was over, we all went through the most beautiful induction ceremony. My mother had traveled back to my college to 'pin' me. My godmothers, both members of the sorority, were there too. It was a happy time, and it was a sad time. The estrangement between me and my line sisters did not just go away. I almost hated the Big Sisters who had been so mean through our pledge period. I knew that I did not want to live with those negative thoughts forever.

"If I did not want to live with those painful thoughts, I would have to forgive the Big Sisters under whom I pledged. Following the 'Forgiveness

Process,' I was able to get relief from the bitterness. However, I still have no desire to locate them and restore our relationships. I have moved on. I am now a member of the same graduate chapter as my mother. We are sorors! We attend meetings and other sorority events together. I'm glad I have forgiven. Recently, one of the sorors who was my 'big sister' found me on Facebook. We exchanged pleasantries, and she told me how she admired me for sticking to my convictions. I have forgiven her and may stay in touch. There will have to be more conversations before I can say that the broken relationship is restored. There may or may not be reconciliation."

Warren's Story

"I was a victim of spousal abuse. I was married many years before I realized that I was abused by my wife. I felt that I was just trying to keep the peace when I endured the verbal and emotional abuse. It started right after we were married.

"We were married in a big church wedding. Hundreds of people attended our wedding. I knew I had loved Rachel for years—even in high school. However, each of us had married others and started families of our own. Now we were back together. At least, I thought we were together.

"There were insults hurled at me in private and in front of others. I was humiliated and hurt beyond words. This tiny little woman knew that I would not fight her because I had been taught that men just don't hit women. Over the years of abuse, however, I grew to feel very hostile. In fact, I was so angry that I secretly wished she would die—even if I had to kill her. It was at that point that I realized that I had to leave. I had to leave because if I didn't get away, I would ruin both our lives and many of those around us such as our children, our parents, and our friends. She would be dead. I would be in prison. My family and friends would be in pain and suffer hurt and embarrassment. Hummm! Hatred breeds more hatred. It is contagious.

"It was a blended family that never did really blend. Rachel's children lived with us. I treated them like they were my own. However, I was not allowed to discipline the son. He was a spoiled brat who got everything he asked for. This child was inconsiderate and had no regard for authority. Rachel always referred to him as 'the baby.' This 'baby' was thirteen years old!

"We were married for three years when we separated. There was that one day, when everything came crashing down. We had gone to the lake. I thought that the peaceful sound of the water would provide a wonderful setting in which to talk. We got started talking, and things went sour. In the heat of the conversation, Rachel said, 'I just married you for spite! I don't love you, and I never will.' I was so hurt that I trembled. Thoughts of hurting Rachel or even killing her entered my mind.

"Immediately, I moved to a different city. I left behind all my worldly goods, but I stuffed the hatred and bitterness into my heart and carried it with me to my new home. I am starting over. I have met some wonderful people through the church that I attend. Eventually, I joined this wonderful church and began to study the Bible more. Sometimes I just read passages of scripture that I select randomly, but it is always helpful to read that I am loved.

"I am now learning to forgive Rachel's behavior. Each time I think of an incident, I go through the Forgiveness Process. There are so many things that happened. It's a good thing not to try to forgive the person all at once. One incident at a time seems to be working for me. I know that I do not want to restore the relationship because I recently asked Rachel about it and she said, 'Not now.' I didn't press her.

"I will probably always love Rachel, but I cannot single-handedly restore our relationship. Using the Forgiveness Process, I do forgive the things she did to me—one at a time. I thank God for the gift of forgiveness."

Gloria's Story

"I thought we were friends. It really hurt when I found out that we must not have been. I had poured my heart into our friendship. Here, she lay dying. The leukemia had taken its painful toll on her body. It took almost two years for this wicked disease to snatch the life out of Van's body. Because of the many efforts to save Van's life, it was just devastating to know that all the hopes we had shared were not fulfilled. I'll have to tell you the full story in order for you to understand how I felt. I want to start at the beginning, but the end really defined our relationship better.

"Van and I met on her first day as the programmer in the Information Technology Department of our international company. We shared a cubicle and many long hours designing, coding, and debugging programs for the new Information Systems computer. Van was a very good programmer whose code went into testing and into production with very few rewrites. Since I had been with the company a few years longer than Van, I took the time to explain the business processes used at our company. I was better at understanding job requirements. Van was better than almost anyone else at converting those conceptual designs into executable programs. We worked together to guide a project all the way through the steps of cost-justification, design, coding, unit testing, stress testing, training, and implementation of the project. I thought we were a good team.

"Every time a new project request came to me, I asked Van to tell me how much time it would take her to code and test the project. She was very accurate, so I trusted her estimates a lot and I counted on her to lead her program coding team through completion of the project. I trusted her. When I found out that Van was sick unto death, it hit me like a ton of bricks.

"Naturally, I was upset that Van was dying, but a new revelation came to me also: You see, I felt that Van had not trusted me with information about her condition and how the leukemia had progressed. It most certainly felt like she did not trust me. I was doubly hurt. Right at the point of her death, I felt betrayed. True, there was nothing I could do about turning back the malicious killer that snatched her life, but if we were truly friends, why had she not included me and held me closer to her heart? Maybe I could have helped her in some other small way. I was hurt and angry. Maybe I was angry because I was hurt. I knew these feelings were more than just the normal grief from losing a friend.

"I felt that I lost a friend and at the same time lost a past history full of what now looked like false memories. I decided to use the Forgiveness Process. It took a long time to work through all the different things that hurt me about Van's death and the 'friendship' I thought we had before her death. Using the Forgiveness Process, I am emerging from that despair. I have the process and the power to forgive! I'm using that power to overcome these and other hurts."

The Forgiveness Process

1. **Separate the person from what they did.**
2. **Realize that the relationship is broken.**
3. **Admit your loss and allow yourself to grieve.**
4. **Try to understand the other person.**
5. **Think of individual acts of violation.**
6. **Start throwing out the junk.**
7. **Guard your heart and mind**

Gloria's Exercise in Forgiving

Following the steps of the Forgiveness Process, Gloria started on her journey of forgiveness. It was not a comfortable journey because Gloria did not see where she might have played a part in the hurt and pain she was suffering. She just felt like she had been wronged and that was that. We started and went step-by-step through the process. Those steps are recorded here, but this is only a synopsis. The discussions, the crying, and the eventual emerging as a victor took some time. Gloria was anxious for freedom from the hatred she was developing for Van, so we started.

1. Separate the person from what they did.

"Van was a person. She was not the leukemia. Van did not let me know that she was dying. That's what Van did. She did not tell me. I could still love Van regardless what she did. I did not have to like everything she did in order to love her. Now I was not divided in my feelings. I was free to love Van completely, but I hated the mistrust and omission from her deepest secrets. However, now I could begin to see the relationship for what it was—broken! It hurt so much, but I knew the relationship did not feel good for me anymore. It was broken."

2. Realize that the relationship is broken.

"It was painful to realize that the relationship was not what I thought it had been. Certainly, because of death the relationship did not exist anymore, but my realization came in that hospital room as Van lay dying. Van had not trusted me with the information of her impending demise. She knew it and had not told me. We did not have the relationship that I thought we had. The relationship was broken. As I faced this painful realization that the relationship that I thought we had was nonexistent. I started to grieve not only for Van's death, but also for feeling so left out of her life." The Forgiveness Coach said that I was ready for step 3 in the Forgiveness Process.

3. Admit your loss and allow yourself to grieve.

"I could not share my grief with anyone for fear that they would think I was being selfish—just feeling sorry for myself. I didn't talk with anyone about my feelings, but I sure know how I felt. Wow! How could Van go and leave me with these broken pieces of a relationship? I cried for the loss and I cried about the 'betrayal' of a friend."

"Once I had done step 1 and step 2, I could go through step 3 as often as I needed because now Van was separate from the acts and nothing else could break the relationship because it was already broken. Whenever I would remember something about Van, I was reminded that she did not trust me and I grieved all over again."

"I allowed myself to have my feelings. Feelings can't be wrong anyway. They may be distorted, but they can't be right or wrong. No longer ashamed of my feelings about Van's leaving me out of a very important part of her life. I was ready to move on to the step 4 in the Forgiveness Process."

4. Try to understand the other person.

"My challenge in this step is to try to understand Van. This is a very important step because to this point, I had been thinking only of myself and how I felt betrayed by Van. It was so hard because I didn't really want to understand Van. I really wanted to go with the concept of Van that I had formulated in my mind. Nevertheless, I looked back at other times. Van never did really share her personal life with those of us at work—including me. She was a rather private individual. At her funeral, her sister had remarked that Van sure did 'suffer in silence' a lot. Her sister was not talking to me. I overheard this crucial piece of the puzzle of understanding Van. Also, when I look back, I can see that I did so much of the talking that it seemed like we were carrying on these great conversations. In truth, Van said very little. I must have taken her silence for agreement and trusted friendship."

"After the funeral, I decided to talk with two of Van's sisters. Van was from a rather large family. She had two brothers and five sisters. Also, two of her cousins lived with them. When Van was living at home, there was always a lot of activity around their home. Both of Van's sisters told me that Van was always quiet. One time, she had the flu that went into pneumonia before Van said anything about being really sick beyond having chills and fever. Van's sisters seemed happy to talk about Van. Perhaps it was part of the way they healed too. Van's younger brother joined the conversation with saying, 'Well really, how could anyone get a word in edgewise when Dad was so loud. Also, Dad was always right, so there was no need trying to interrupt him.' They all laughed."

"We talked all through the reception that followed the burial. I could tell that they truly loved Van and found no fault with her personality. Someone even mentioned how smart she was in high school and college. Both times, Van graduated at the top of her class. Mostly, I just listened to this enlightenment, but I did tell how much her work was appreciated. With that statement, I realized that I had not shown any true interest in Van's personal life. We were business associates. When I started to understand Van better, I guess I didn't take it so personally anymore. I could really stop here, but the Forgiveness Coach encouraged me to continue to the next step in the Forgiveness Process."

5. Think of individual acts of violation.

"I had built up quite an inventory of ways that I thought Van had betrayed me. My mind had done some 'skip-to-the-loo' thinking. I went from thinking about Van's not telling me about the seriousness of the leukemia all the way to wondering what else she could have been hiding from me. When I learned more about Van, it was almost easy to start to overcome the hurtful residue from feeling so betrayed. Yes, I thought I was more important in her life, but perhaps she was trying to spare me the worrying that she knew I would do. The feelings of betrayal, whether real or imaginary, had to go! I was ready to move on to step 7 of the Forgiveness Process."

6. Start throwing out the junk.

If Gloria could throw out the junk that had accumulated in her heart, she would be free! Throwing out the junk is the actual act of forgiveness. Out of forgiveness comes healing. For the feeling of being betrayed or not trusted enough to share her pain, Gloria thought about just that—not about Van. As she thought about being betrayed or not trusted, she cried. The shock of learning that Van was leaving all too soon made Gloria angry with her. However, as her Forgiveness Coach, I helped Gloria understand that her anger was a natural part of grieving and she might really have been masking other feelings such as hurt. Gloria responded, "I was also angry with myself for not being more sensitive. I hated those ugly feelings. The bitterness and the resentment were dragging me down. My relationships with others at work suffered. I was grouchy, depressed, blaming myself for not seeing what was happening to Van. I thought of how I was feeling and decided that I didn't want to feel that way anymore." We prayed together and she asked God to take away the pain, the anxiety, depression, and insecurity. Gloria cried and laughed at the same time.

"I cried as I allowed God to fill me with love for Van and to celebrate her life. Van was a beautiful person and she did not owe me a thing. In the process, I also got more love for myself. After all, I had shared myself with another human being. My love for others does not depend on how they show their love for me. This cleansing did not take place all at once. As time passed, if I thought of other things Van did not share with me, I stopped right away to forgive—to completely let go of those negative things.

7. Guard your heart and mind.

The Forgiveness Coach said, "For the rest of your life, there will be events that will happen not to your choosing. People may say or do things that you think are aimed at hurting you. Here is where you stop and remember that whatever comes your way, the choice to let in hurt, bitterness, pain, or resentment is up to you. Make a conscious choice to guard your heart and your mind. It's definitely a process to get rid of unforgiveness! You can do this! You must remember the steps in the Forgiveness Process and apply these steps immediately. As you learn to apply these steps quickly, you don't allow stressful stuff to permeate your mind, your body, your spirit! There is an old saying that 'An ounce of prevention is worth a pound of cure.' Better to guard your being from unforgiveness because the prevention of unforgiveness is much easier thing than going for the cure. Hurray! You can forgive and will carry this skill throughout your life. You can also teach others to get free."

Andrew's Story

> *Jeremy was very strong willed. He thought his superior intellect entitled him to always be in control. One fateful night, he would commit his last strong-willed act. Now his father, Andrew, is bitter and unforgiving.*

Andrew's story is really Jeremy's story. But Jeremy is not alive to tell his story. You should have known Jeremy: he was life itself. Very intelligent and not a bit humble, Jeremy was a very headstrong young man. In fact, he was sort of arrogant. Jeremy lived with his dad and went to the local university where he played on the rugby team. In his college classes, Jeremy constantly challenged the professors with his loaded questions. Jeremy asked questions in such a way as to let one know that he already knew the answer to his own question. It was not the answers that Jeremy was seeking. Jeremy seemed to be seeking center stage. In spite of his brashness, Jeremy was well liked because he always exhibited a love for people even if he thought that they were not as bright as he.

Jeremy had a few close friends. They boosted each other's egos in intellectual discussions that solved nothing. Jeremy was the leader of the pack. It was almost like Jeremy was president of the Club with complete veto power and always the final say, always the last word.

One night after a party where Jeremy had too much to drink, his car left the road and he was killed. After his body was cut from the wreckage, it was obvious even to the nonmedical bystanders that Jeremy was dead. Jeremy was taken to a local hospital about twenty miles away. At the hospital, he was pronounced dead. The family members were notified to come to the hospital.

Jeremy's father, Andrew, was first to arrive at the hospital. Jeremy was still in a treatment suite in the emergency room where Andrew was politely told that Jeremy has died without suffering. Andrew was in shock. The staff at the hospital asked if Andrew wanted them to call anyone. Andrew had them call Jeremy's mother, his sister, and his stepmother. Soon they were all there and formed a circle of devastated mourners.

Andrew made arrangements for Jeremy's funeral, which was held at the church where Jeremy had first been introduced to church as a child. It was a bright day and people filled up the small church. When a young person dies, usually the funeral is very well attended. This was no exception. Jeremy's friends attended and cried unashamedly because they had just lost the strong president of the club.

Andrew watched Jeremy's friends grieving at Jeremy's funeral. After the accident, Andrew had asked them why no one took the keys from Jeremy before he started driving home after drinking so much. They had told Andrew that Jeremy would not let anyone drive him. This was not a good answer as far as Andrew was concerned. They should have *taken* his keys away from him. Now they grieve at the loss of their friend! Andrew was angry and blamed them all the more. He said that he could never forgive them for letting his son drive drunk.

Daily, it seems Andrew talks to someone about his son's death. Andrew seems to become more and more convinced that Jeremy's friends should have done more to save Jeremy. In his anger, Andrew said that, "It should have been them rather than my son!" Although anger is one of the natural steps of grieving, Andrew has allowed his feelings to progress beyond anger to bitterness and resentment.

Andrew's Exercise in Forgiving

Following the steps of the Forgiveness Process, Andrew skeptically started on his journey to forgive Jeremy's friends for Jeremy's untimely death. It was not an easy journey for a number of reasons. The most strangling reason was because Andrew did not at all blame Jeremy. I don't know why. Perhaps it was because if he had held Jeremy responsible, Andrew would have had to take a look at self too. Why didn't he teach Jeremy to more readily to accept the advice of others? As far back as he could remember, Jeremy was headstrong.

Everyone said that Jeremy was a lot like his dad. Andrew took this as a compliment. Now Jeremy was gone and Andrew blamed anyone else other than Jeremy or himself. Andrew's journey to forgiveness will be especially hard until he looks at himself and at Jeremy. We started and went step by step through the process. Summaries of those steps are recorded here. The discussions were especially trying since Andrew was so sure that he was right to blame Jeremy's friends for Jeremy's death. Nevertheless, as his Forgiveness Coach, I helped him go through the process step by step.

1. Separate the person from what they did.

"Jeremy's friends, Freddy and Tony, had allowed Jeremy to leave the party drunk. These three young people had been friends since the start of middle school. All three played on the same soccer teams and the same basketball teams. Freddy and Tony spent a lot of time at our house. It was hard, but I started to look at what they did separately from who they were. Once I separated them from the act, I was free to love Jeremy's young friends again. I hated what they did or what I thought they did to me. I did not want to see them, however. Now I could begin to see the relationship for what it was—broken!"

2. Realize that the relationship is broken.

"It was painful to realize that the relationship that I had with Tony and Freddy was not strong enough to have saved Jeremy. We did not have the relationship that I thought we had. The relationship was broken. As I faced this painful realization that the relationship that I thought we had, I started to grieve not only for Jeremy's death, but also for the loss of the trust I had in Jeremy's friends. Once I knew that the relationship that I thought I had with Jeremy's friends was broken, I was ready for step 3 in the Forgiveness Process."

3. Admit your loss and allow yourself to grieve.

"I cannot begin to explain the depth of my grief. My pain for the loss of Jeremy was so great that I did not want to live. Eventually, I looked for where to place the blame. I've always been a logical person. This time, however, logic did not get me too far. Even though I blamed Tony and Freddy, Jeremy was just as dead. Besides, two of the people who loved Jeremy best were not there to share my grief. Oh, how I wished they understood! Well, I came to realize that I missed Jeremy's friends too. It was almost like they left my life when Jeremy left this life. I did not understand Freddy and Tony, and I almost hated them for continuing to live after Jeremy is gone. They still see the morning sun, whereas Jeremy never will again. I almost hated them. Yes. That's it. I have such strong negative feelings toward them. Then I remembered that in step 1 of the Forgiveness Process, I had separated Freddy and Tony from what they did. What I really hated was their letting Jeremy leave the party drunk. It's a process, but when I realized that I missed Tony and Freddy, I was ready to move on."

4. Try to understand the other person.

"Here is where I was coached to try to understand Jeremy's friends. This is a very hard step for me because I had no desire to try to understand them. I didn't really want to understand them at all. I just wanted them to die in Jeremy's place. Then one day at the grocery store, a neighbor asked me how Tony and Freddy were taking the death of their very well loved friend. I really had not stopped to think how they must be feeling. As a matter of fact, I gave a very curt answer right there in Aisle 5 of the local grocery store. I said, 'I don't care how they feel. They should have taken the keys away from Jeremy so that he could not drive drunk.' The neighbor quietly said that they had been drunk too. Their judgment was just as impaired as Jeremy's, but they did not happen to get killed that night. She did say that she heard that they are grieving so hard that one of them has dropped out of school and is under a doctor's care. She couldn't remember whether it was Tony or Freddy who was hospitalized briefly for a break down.

"As I left the store, I thought about those boys and how much I missed their being at our house with Jeremy. As a result of my neighbor's information, I started to understand that Freddy and Tony were hurting too. I missed them, but I was not ready to let them back into my life. As far as I was concerned, the relationship was still broken. I want to feel better. If this forgiveness stuff will help, I'm giving it a try."

5. Think of individual acts of violation.

"Jeremy's friends were guilty of one thing. They always let Jeremy have his way. If that is a violation to me, then I am just as much to blame as they are. I always thought of Jeremy as a natural born leader and that others were right to follow him. Well, there really is no need to fix blame in this situation. I was ready to move on to the next steps."

6. Start throwing out the junk.

"Perhaps I was angry with myself for not teaching Jeremy to listen to others with respect for what is right. I cried. I cried some more. The Forgiveness Coach said that I should pray and ask God to remove the pain, the anxiety, depression, insecurity resulting from those happenings. I cried as I asked, 'Where was God when Jeremy needed Him?' Patiently, the Forgiveness Coach said, 'God was right there with Jeremy, but Jeremy had taken matters into his own hands. God will not violate our wills. However, God loved Jeremy even with his head strong attitude. God still loves Jeremy and God loves you too. Forgive those boys. They were Jeremy's friends. Jeremy would not want you to be bitter toward them.' I do forgive them, but I do not want them back in my life just yet."

7. Guard your heart and mind.

The Forgiveness Coach led me through this step. She said, "For the rest of your life, there will be events that will happen not to your liking. People will say or do things that bring hurt, anger, or humiliation to you. You have a choice right then! Stop and remember that whatever comes your way, the choice to let in feelings of betrayal, being left out, bitterness, pain, or resentment is up to you. Choose to guard your heart and mind. You can do this! Remember the steps in the Forgiveness Process and apply these steps right away. As you learn to apply these steps quickly, you will find that you do not allow somebody else's stuff to permeate your mind, your body, or your spirit! After all, as was in the case with Jeremy's friends, the other people may not be doing something to you at all!" Guard your heart and mind.

JoAnna's Story

JoAnna thought she had found true happiness. She was getting back on her feet after a bitter divorce in another state. She left behind the abusive man who had been her husband and who was the stepfather of her two girls. When she met Dick, JoAnna was delighted that he was so charming.

Dick swept JoAnna off her feet, and she was delighted that he seemed to love the girls too. Dick had an evil side. He was into pornography and pedophilia. When little Amy said that she and Dick "played games" where Dick touched her "girly part," JoAnna just knew that Dick had molested her daughter. JoAnna confronted Dick with the accusation. Dick denied everything and even cried real tears in telling his story. He said that Amy must have misunderstood and that he would never do anything to harm the girls. Once more, JoAnna succumbed to Dick's charms.

One day, JoAnna came back from the store and found Dick in bed with Amy. Amy was naked. Dick had turned on some pornographic movies for the two of them to watch. JoAnna walked in on this nauseating scene and snatched little Amy away. Then she came back to confront Dick. This time, there was no way JoAnna could believe anything but her eyes. Dick became very angry and told JoAnna that he would kill her and her girls if she told anyone. Dick was hostile, yet tearful. JoAnna was afraid of him. She recognized violence and abuse from her prior experience. When Dick tried to grab at her, JoAnna took out a gun and shot Dick. He died before the police got there. Immediately, JoAnna asked herself what she had done. She thought about her two little girls having to be placed in a home while their mother was in prison for murder. JoAnna was arrested.

During the long months before her trial, JoAnna did a lot of thinking. She was truly sorry for taking a human life, but she was glad her children were away from the molestation. JoAnna looked back over her life and thought she should have heeded the "red flags" that she had seen along the way. Amy had told JoAnna about the "games" she and Dick played. Amy was only three years old, so she could not have made up lies about molestation. Dick always wanted to spend time with Amy alone. Amy started having trouble sleeping and stated that she was afraid to go into her room alone at night. There were several signs along the way. JoAnna beat herself up with guilt. JoAnna hated Dick so much. Thoughts of Dick haunted JoAnna's every waking moment. In addition to the guilt of not protecting Amy, JoAnna was consumed with hatred for Dick. Regardless how her case would be decided at her trial, JoAnna wanted to get rid of the bitterness. Her spirit was vexed.

Naturally, JoAnna wanted to think that Amy would not remember the trauma, but she knew better. She knew that Amy would need professional counseling to get over the violations. JoAnna wanted to be forgiven by God, by Dick's family, by the State of Nevada, and by Amy. However, the things that stayed with her to the point of making her sick were the hatred and bitterness, the revulsion, and the pain of remembering Dick's ugly ways. JoAnna knew that she would have to forgive this animal so that she did not give him her power even in his death. JoAnna started through the Forgiveness Process.

JoAnna's Exercise in Forgiving

Following the steps of the Forgiveness Process, JoAnna started on her journey to forgive Dick. It was not an easy journey for a number of reasons. Nevertheless, we went through the process step by step.

1. Separate the person from what they did.

"Dick had abused my daughter and betrayed my trust. These are the things that kept JoAnna thinking about the past: the abuse, the sexual molestation, the snatching of innocence from her child. Dick was gone, but the memory of the things he did lingered to embitter JoAnna. Once I could separate Dick from what he did, I could see that the relationship had not been good for a long time. I should have investigated my suspicions. I could begin to see the relationship for what it was—broken!"

2. Realize that the relationship is broken.

"It was easy to realize that the relationship had been broken long before Dick's death. Looking back, I wondered if we ever had a good relationship. I thought we did, but I must have been wrong. Dick could not have molested Amy if he really loved me. If we had a good relationship at one time, it was not there when he molested my daughter. We did not have the relationship that I thought we had.

"Yes, the relationship was gone, never to be restored. As I faced this painful realization, I wondered when Dick had stopped loving me. Did he ever love me? I started to grieve over the sudden losses: the death of the man I had once loved and the loss of my daughter's innocence. I was grieving over many things at once. Once I realized my relationship with Dick had been broken, I went into a tailspin about all that happened."

3. Admit your loss and allow yourself to grieve.

"Since I blamed myself for not catching the situation earlier, I also thought of myself as a bad mom. I cannot begin to convey the depth of my grief. My pain was so deep that I could not think straight. To be truthful, I felt really bad about taking Dick's life. I grieved so hard over Amy's hurts. She had tried to tell me, but I did not put it all together. I kept denying my feelings at first.

"I had killed a man, yet I just wanted things to be all right. That's crazy. Things were not right. I could not make things right for me or Amy . . . or Dick, so I hurt. I hurt so bad that I didn't care what happened to me. I was going to jail and my girls would have to face the future without me. My thoughts were so jumbled. When I realized that I missed Dick and the future that we planned together, I felt guilty about missing him.

"I felt so bad about everything. I couldn't eat. I couldn't sleep. When I did try to sleep, I had bad dreams about trying to plug the bullet hole in Dick so that I would not be a murderer. I had bad dreams about Amy's pain and her fear about being killed or having her mommy killed. I am really grieving for Amy more than I am for myself. I don't know how I'll do it, but both of my girls need counseling right away. They have been abandoned by so many of the grown-ups they trusted. I grieved hard! The Forgiveness Coach said that I need to try to understand the perpetrator—Dick. Reluctantly, I started on step 4."

4. Try to understand the other person.

"In this step, I will try to understand Dick. I really did not want to understand him at first. I stated that I did not even want to think about him. Much less, I did not feel the need to understand him. The Forgiveness Coach told me that this is a very important step because it gets me out of myself and broadens my thinking. It was so hard. In an effort to understand Dick, I wanted to turn to Dick's family, but I didn't dare.

"I was repulsed by Dick, and I sure did not understand him. What happened to him? Where was his pride and self-esteem? How could he do this to 'our' child? I talked with a counselor named Gordon. Gordon helped me understand Dick a little more. I learned that Dick was a pedophile and was probably a victim of some form of sexual abuse in his childhood. Gordon said that pedophiles generally appear to be trustworthy and respectable. Male pedophiles often marry women with little children. Pedophiles find different ways and places to be alone with children and gradually 'groom' them through trust and friendliness.

"Somewhere along the way, I realized that I, too, was taken in by Dick's winning ways. I learned that pedophilia is a mental illness and that as a pedophile Dick would not stop on his own accord. They do not take responsibility for their behavior and deny that they're doing anything harmful. As crazy as it sounded to me, Dick did not think he was doing any harm to Amy. He would have gone on abusing until caught. He was caught. He is dead.

"Although I did not feel the least bit sorry for him, I began to understand him more. I understood now that he was not doing something to intentionally hurt us. He was suffering too. I did not like what he did and if her were alive, I would never want to see him again.

However, I understood him better after the counseling. Poor Amy. Poor Dick. Poor me."

5. Think of individual acts of violation.

"I thought of things real and imaginary that Dick had done. To my way of thinking, in his selfish, sick way, Dick had betrayed my trust. I trusted him to be alone with 'our' girls. He betrayed that trust. He robbed Amy of her innocence. He lied to my face. There were lesser acts of violation too, but the molestation of my daughter and the betrayal loomed so large in my mind that I decided to concentrate on these acts."

6. Start throwing out the junk.

"The Forgiveness Coach said that if I could throw out the junk that had accumulated in my heart, I would be free to forgive Dick and move on to deal with other issues in life. A little bit at a time was all that I was willing to deal with. Although in jail for killing Dick, I was imprisoned emotionally because I had taken a human life. No matter what the law says, I felt guilty already. I would serve an emotional life sentence for killing someone.

"I was emotionally imprisoned because I had failed to provide safety for my child. All that emotional baggage kept me bound to the past and what happened. I needed to throw out the junk of guilt, self-hatred, loathing of Dick, and total embarrassment about what had gone on at my house. I felt betrayed by Dick. Why didn't he love me enough to leave my daughter alone? Then I remembered: Dick was a pedophile. He was a sick man. In his sickness, he really could not even love himself. As I realized the truth of this statement, I let go of the feeling of not being worthy of Dick's love. I was worthy.

"Whenever I think of other things that Dick did that hurt me, I will begin right away to forgive that incident so that I do not continue to hurt. Besides, I want to be forgiven by God for the things I had done. I knew that I could not go to God and ask Him to forgive me if I don't forgive others, including Dick. It's hard work, really hard, but I will keep throwing out the junk as long as necessary."

7. Guard your heart and mind.

"I repeat after the Forgiveness Coach, 'I can do this!' I will recall the steps in the Forgiveness Process and apply these steps right away. Forgiveness is a process, and I can choose to let in anger, hurt, bitterness, and other junk of unforgiveness. I choose to guard my heart and my mind. It's definitely a process to get rid of stuff! I agree with the Forgiveness Coach that forgiveness is a valuable life skill. I understand that things will continue to happen that I do not like, but I have a choice to let junk into my heart or to guard against it."

Jennifer's Story

"I thought I had forgiven Eldora. I had not heard from her in such a long time. As a result of a broken relationship, Eldora was gone from my life. It was through a mutual acquaintance that she came back into my life. It had been many years since I last saw her.

"Eldora had started a successful leg of a multilevel marketing business. I was in her 'down line' and was largely responsible for her doing so well. I watched Eldora's attitude change as she became more and more successful. I dismissed her arrogance as being the characteristic of one who is newly rich. Eldora became rich. When she became mean and refused to share, however, I left the business. I was getting nothing out of it but was spending lots of time making Eldora rich. I was tremendously hurt by the change in our relationship. In fact, we no longer had a good relationship. We had a broken relationship.

"Now a luncheon invitation had brought us together again. During the luncheon, Eldora made a very emotional talk about the past. She stated, 'I just looked around and you were gone from my life!' Eldora's speech made me ill. I never heard her say that she was sorry for what she may have contributed toward the breakup of our relationship. I only heard her statement that I deserted her. This felt like an accusation to me. I was ever so hurt.

"I was hurt because Eldora's little talk seemed to blame me for everything. I felt that others who were listening to her speak and perceived that I had betrayed poor little Eldora. I felt betrayed, again. The same feelings of hurt, anger, and bitterness that I thought were gone were back again to haunt me. This time, I realized that I must go through the forgiveness process to be rid of the 'trash' in my heart."

Note: As Forgiveness Coach for Jennifer, I took her through the Forgiveness Process and felt that she understood it. She said that she wanted to think about it a little longer. Maybe she was just not ready to forgive Eldora. In a case like this, Jennifer may need some professional counseling because although her case may not seem earth-shattering to anyone else, there were other deeper issues in Jennifer's life.

Alison's Story

Linda was the eldest of seven children. She was a typical eldest child; responsible, smart, and dependable. As she grew older, her parents depended on her to look after her younger siblings. This included helping with homework, ironing their clothes, and cooking meals. She became the emergency adult when her parents were at work.

As Linda and her siblings became adults, Linda's role as the emergency adult became real. When the Army drafted two of her brothers into the Army during the Vietnam conflict, Linda purchased life insurance policies for them and named their mother as the beneficiary. Linda also helped her siblings by loaning them money to pay their bills or helping them when they were in trouble.

There was one sibling Linda helped more than most. It was her brother Ronald. Ronald was 15 years younger than Linda, and due to their age difference, Linda practically raised him. He looked up to her and depended on her. Ronald enlisted in the Army and served a four-year stint. When he returned home, Ronald had a hard time finding a job. Linda suggested he join the Army Reserves so he could earn a paycheck and learn a new skill. Ronald didn't listen and drifted from one dead-end job to another. Ronald attended the local technical school and studied construction management. He didn't finish the program and again found gainful employment difficult to obtain. Ronald eventually became addicted to drugs and dealt with addiction most of his adult life. The addiction caused him to have a hard time staying employed and made it difficult to support his family.

Over 20 years, Linda bailed Ronald out of jail and helped his family survive by purchasing groceries and paying bills. When Ronald and his wife divorced, he went through periods of homelessness and incarceration. After release from prison, Ronald lived with Linda off and on for over ten years.

When Linda became ill, Ronald was still living with her. He was helpful around the house but never found gainful employment. All the time Ronald lived with his sister, he never once said "thank you" or apologized for his behavior. Linda never stopped loving her brother and forgave him without an apology. In her mind, Linda was doing what she thought she should do as Ronald's sister and love him unconditionally. That's what Granny taught her children, so Linda believed she was honoring Granny by not expecting an apology, but forgiving her brother for what he did to her. However, Linda's daughter, Alison, was tremendously hurt feeling that her mom was being used to support Uncle Ronald.

Alison's Exercise in Forgiving

Alison talked to the Forgiveness Coach about her hurt and anger about Uncle Ronald's behavior. The Forgiveness Coach asked a few questions. One question asked if Alison was angry with her mother or her uncle, or both. Alison was very clear that she was not angry with her mom, but she was very hurt by Uncle Ronald for taking and never giving. Uncle Ronald was much older than Alison. Alison said she felt used by Uncle Ronald, a mam twice her age. After about seven months, Alison gave Uncle Ronald a date by which he had to be gone. She put him out. After he was gone, Alison was still bitter about the whole thing. Guided by the Forgiveness Coach, Alison's journey to forgive Uncle Ronald began. It was not a comfortable journey for many reasons. Nevertheless, she went through the process step by step, and this is her story in her own words..

1. Separate the person from what they did.
"Uncle Ronald had taken advantage of my mom and did not seem to care. He never said words of appreciation, and I did not like him. He did not try to support himself. He just came into our house as though my mom owed him a good living. Uncle Ronald took resources from my mom that would have made her life better. And when my mom passed away, I took over all payments – even the mortgage. Now, Uncle

Ronald became the albatross around my neck, so to speak. I did not like his actions. I had always liked my uncle, but I could not see myself as his support system. After a short time, I became angry about providing him a living with no thanks and no effort to help meet the expenses of the household. I did not like what he did!!! Once I could separate Uncle Ronald from what he did, I could see that the relationship had not been good. I had been affected by Uncle Ronald's sponging off my mom and now he was sponging off me. As for my relationship with Uncle Ronald, I could see the relationship for what it was—not good. It was broken!"

2. Realize that the relationship is broken.

"It was easy to realize that my relationship with Uncle Ronald was broken. I hated him! Uncle Ronaldwould not have taken advantage of my mom if he really loved her. If my mom and he had a good relationship at one time, it was not there when he took so much from her.

Uncle Ronald would also say mean things to mom about her cooking or other provisions. Although my mom did not seem to care how much she gave to her brother, I really hated that he took so much and gave nothing, not even a 'Thank you' to my mom or me."

"Yes, my relationship with Uncle Ronald was gone, never to be restored. As I faced this painful realization, I wondered when Uncle Ronald had stopped loving me. Did my uncle ever love me? I started to grieve over the sudden realization of my loss. I was grieving over many things at once. Once I realized my relationship with Uncle Ronaldwas broken, I went into a tailspin about all that had been done to enable Uncle Ronald to take advantage of my mom and me."

3. Admit your loss and allow yourself to grieve.

"Since I blamed myself for not standing strong andputting Uncle Ronald out earlier, I became angrier and more bitter. Was I weak? Had I allowed myself to be an unwilling caregiver to a grown, healthy man? A man who made ugly unnecessary remarks to me. I cannot begin to convey the depth of my anger. My pain was so deep that I could not think straight. To be truthful, I felt really bad about puttingUncle

Ronald out. I was confused and depressed. I told myself I had done the right thing, so why did I feel so bad? I kept denying my feelings at first. I tried telling myself that what I did was the best thing for Uncle Ronald. Or was it? I felt guilty because I thought maybe my mom would have been unhappy. I hurt. My thoughts were so jumbled. When I realized that I missed Uncle Ronald, I felt guilty about missing him.

"I felt so bad about everything. The Forgiveness Coach helped me realize I was grieving and taught me that it was normal to grieve. Grieving could not be explained as an intellectual matter. It is a heart matter. I should allow myself to grieve even though I did not understand. I grieved hard! The Forgiveness Coach said that I need to try to understand the perpetrator—Uncle Ronald. Reluctantly, I started on the next step – Step 4."

4. Try to understand the other person.

"In this step, I will try to understand Uncle Ronald. In reality, I did not want to understand him at first. I thought of him as a worthless and wicked man. I did not even want to think about him. Even more, I did not feel the need to understand him. The Forgiveness Coach told me that this is an essential step because it gets me out of myself and broadens my thinking. It was so hard. In trying to understand Uncle Ronald, I wanted to turn to Uncle Ronald and ask him why he never told my Mom how much he appreciated her. I just did not like Uncle Ronald, and I sure did not understand him. What happened to him? Where were his pride and self-esteem? He acted like a child who expected to be cared for as a dependent.

"Then, I remembered what my mom had told me. Mom was the eldest of seven children when Granny died. My mom became the woman in charge of the home – cooking the meals for her dad and her younger siblings, laundering the clothes, helping with homework, getting the younger siblings to school, teaching them to say their prayers as she tucked them in bed each night. Uncle Ronald was the youngest – the baby. Wow! He was Mom's child by default.

"Although I did not feel sorry for him, I began to understand him more. I understood now that he was not doing something to take advantage of us. He was suffering too. I did not like what he did, but I would look for him at family gatherings. I understood him better after the Forgiveness Coach's counseling. Poor Uncle Ronald. Poor me."

5. Think of individual acts of violation.

"I thought of things real and imaginary that Uncle Ronald had done. In his selfish, childish way, Uncle Ronald had betrayed my trust in my way of thinking. I trusted him to be as grown as he looked. Uncle Ronald betrayed that trust. He took from my mom and never gave her the thanks she deserved. Mom provided all his meals, bought him some of his clothes and gave him money many times."

6. Start throwing out the junk.

"The Forgiveness Coach said that if I could throw out the junk that had accumulated in my heart, I would be free to forgive Uncle Ronald and move on to deal with other issues in life. All I was willing to deal with was a small amount at a time. The junk in my heart made me spiritually and emotionally stymied until I started asking God to help me get the junk out of my heart. The Forgiveness Coach said, "Another word for "junk" is "sin," and God can take away that sin. Ask Him to forgive you for taking in the hurt and bitterness and other negative feelings. Coach called it emotional baggage and explained that emotional baggage kept me bound to the past because its weight is too heavy. I needed to throw out the junk of hatred, guilt, and loathing of Uncle Ronald. Then I remembered, Uncle Ronald had never taken care of himself. He had the kind of personality thatmakes people want to be around him. Sometimes his dry sense of humor takes people by surprise. He appears quiet, but he participates well in conversation. However, Uncle Ronald could not hold onto a job. He was a loser! He did not seem to love himself. As I realized this statement's truth, I let go of the feeling of not being loved or respected byUncle Ronald.

"Whenever I think of other things that Uncle Ronald did that hurt me, I will begin right away to forgive that incident so that I do not continue to hurt. Besides, I want to be forgiven by God for the things I had done. I knew that I could not go to God and ask Him to forgive me if I don't forgive others, including Uncle Ronald. It's hard work, really hard, but I will keep throwing out the junk as long as necessary." I must not let anything get into my heart and mind that does not help me love me. I must guard my heart and mind.

7. **Guard your heart and mind.**
The Forgiveness Coach had me repeat the following phrases:
- I can do this!
- I will recall the steps in the Forgiveness Process.
- I will apply these steps right away.
- Forgiveness is a process.
- I can choose to let in anger, hurt, bitterness, and other junk.
- I can forgive or live with unforgiveness. My choice.
- Unforgiveness is crippling. It's a sin

I choose to guard my heart and mind. It's a process to get rid of stuff! I agree with the Forgiveness Coach that forgiveness is a valuable life skill. I understand that things will continue to happen that I do not like, but I have a choice to let junk into my heart or to guard against it."

From the Antwon Fisher Movie

An example of a story gleaned from a movie is that of a young man named Antwon Fisher. This is a true story written by Antwon Fisher about his life. Antwon Fisher was born in a women's correctional facility by a mother who abandoned him when she was released. His father has been shot and killed two months before Antwon was born. Antwon Fisher grew up in a foster home where there was much abuse. He became a very angry young man who trusted nobody. Having nowhere to go, Antwon joined the navy and was stationed in California. While in the navy, a counselor took an interest in helping Antwon to overcome his anger by forgiving his family for the abandonment and his foster family for the abuse. Antwon asked why he needed to forgive. The counselor answered, "So you can free yourself."

Through counseling, Antwon was encouraged to find his family and start to mend his heart. Reluctantly, Antwon went to look for his family. He found his father's family who embraced him and showered him with love. He found his mother in a rundown tenement house. He asked her a few questions which remained unanswered. When Antwon returned to California and looked up the counselor. Antwon reported, "I found my mother. In my heart, I forgive her, but if I never see her again, it's all right."

This is a good example of forgiving someone although the broken relationship was not reconciled. Antwon's mother did not show remorse nor repent to Antwon in any way. She simply stared at him. This is a good example of the fact that there is no restoration of the relationship without repentance.

Conclusion

The Forgiveness Process works. Anyone can learn to forgive if willing to go through the steps and ask God to remove the "stuff" accumulated in their hearts. That "stuff" is sin. If we are commanded to love one another, then we must not hate. Hatred, then, is a sin. It is direct disobedience to God's commands. We must stop feeling justified in rehearsing the same old perpetrations and storing up those same old feelings. That is self-destructive.

The destructiveness of unforgiveness has been documented many times over. It causes stress. Stress breaks down the spirit, the body, and the mind. Counselors are beginning to recognize the effects of unforgiveness on the health and well-being of their clients. They are beginning to help clients get away from the hatred, bitterness, loathing of self and others, anger, hurt, and other stressful emotions! They recognize the need for forgiveness. Learn how to forgive! Practice forgiveness! Live and love!

The Forgiveness Process

1 Separate the person from what they did.
2 Realize that the relationship is broken.
3 Admit your loss, allow yourself to grieve.
4 Try to understand the other person.
5 Think of individual acts of violation.
6 Start throwing out the junk.
7 Guard your heart and mind.

Appendix A

**Original quotes and thoughts on forgiveness
by Dr. Julia Frazier White**

⚜

The Power of Reversal
He has taught us forgiveness and the mighty power thereof.
He gave us this gift to undo things that keep us from His love.

⚜

One cannot soar to new heights when held
down by the weight of unforgiveness.

⚜

On the road to Success, unforgiveness is a roadblock.

⚜

When traveling through life, travel light.
Leave out the weight of unforgiveness.

⚜

Forgiving does not erase the memory of the hurt. It erases the hurt.

⚜

Forgiving is the power to create a fresh outlook on life.

⚜

Forgiving is the power to set one's self free.

⚜

Unforgiveness is slavery in its worse form.
There are too many masters to serve.
Some are Hatred, Worthlessness, Bitterness, Fear,
Depression, and Ugliness.
These are unrelenting slave masters.

ട്ട

Unforgiveness keeps us hitched up to the past as
surely as if bridled and tied to a hitching post.

ട്ട

Instead of saying, "Forgive and forget," perhaps
we should say "Forgive then forget."
Or "Forgive to forget." The latter is impossible without the former.

ട്ട

Forgetting is not a brain cramp. It is a decision.

ട്ട

When we forget the pain, it doesn't matter that
we did not forget the incident.
We may not want to forget the incident because the remembrance
of it may keep us from being in the same situation again.

ട്ട

Forgiving is not easy, but it is the easiest way to get back to loving.

ട്ട

Forgive! Forget! Forgo pain! Forever!

ട്ട

Forgiving is a choice. Choose to forgive.

ട്ട

Forgiveness is like the heart cleaning we do before
inviting others into our hearts.

ട്ട

Forgiveness sets the forgiver free—free to live, love, and laugh.

ട്ട

Forgiving breaks the chains that keep one shackled to the past.

ട്ട

Unload the burden of unforgiving. Forgive!

❧

Some coronary events may be prevented by forgiving.

❧

Reclaim your beauty!
I have seen the countenance of forgivers change right before my eyes.
You can give yourself a facelift.
Forgive!

❧

Appendix B

Quotes from Famous People

Forgiveness Quotes

Forgivenessis one of those truths that are recognized across cultural, religious, and other boundaries. When attuned to forgiveness, one finds much on the subject. This appendix includes references to forgiveness from many sources. It shows forgiveness to be a timeless and universal truth.

- ❖ If we really want to love, we must learn how to forgive. (Mother Theresa)

- ❖ Humanity is never so beautiful as when praying for forgiveness, or else forgiving another. (Jean Paul Richter)

- ❖ Genuine forgiveness is participation, reunion overcoming the powers of estrangement . . . We cannot love unless we have accepted forgiveness, and the deeper our experience of forgiveness is the greater is our love. (Paul Tillich)

- ❖ Love is an act of endless forgiveness. (Peter Ustinov)

- ❖ He is the One that accepts repentance from His Servants and forgives sins: and He knows all that ye do. (Koran, Surah 42:25)

- "I can forgive, but I cannot forget" is only another way of saying, I will not forgive. Forgiveness ought to be like a cancelled note—torn in two, and burned up, so that it never can be shown against one. (Henry Ward Beecher)

- Children begin by loving their parents; as they grow older they judge them; sometimes they forgive them. (Oscar Wilde)
- Forgive many things in others; nothing in yourself. (Ausonius)

- It is easier to forgive an enemy than a friend. (Madame Dorothée Deluzy)

- The weak can never forgive. Forgiveness is the attribute of the strong. (Mahatma Gandhi)

- The secret of forgiving everything is to understand nothing. (George Bernard Shaw)

- There is no revenge so complete as forgiveness. (Josh Billings)

- Always forgive your enemies—nothing annoys them so much. (Oscar Wilde)

- To err is human; to forgive, divine. (Alexander Pope)

- A woman who can't forgive should never have more than a nodding acquaintance with a man. (Ed Howe)

- Always forgive your enemies—but never forget their names. (Robert F. Kennedy)

- We cannot forgive, because that means forgetting also. If we forget, then we're doomed, because the past will creep back to poison our future. (John Gardner)

- ❖ Teach us delight in simple things, And fun that has no bitter springs, Forgiveness free of evil done, And love to all beneath the sun. ("Christmas in India" by Rudyard Kipling)

- ❖ And forgive us our debts, as we also have forgiven our debtors. (Matt. 6:12, NRSV)

- ❖ Forgiveness is an embrace, across all barriers, against all odds, in defiance of all that is mean and petty and vindictive and cruel in this life. (Kent Nerburn in *Calm Surrender*)

- ❖ I think it means . . . putting yourself in the position of the other person, and wiping away any sort of resentment and antagonism you feel toward them. (Jimmy Carter, thirty-ninth president of the United States of America, Nobel Peace Prize winner, 2003)

- ❖ Help us, O God of our salvation, for the glory of your name; deliver us, and forgive our sins, for your name's sake. (Ps. 79:9, NRSV)

- ❖ To forgive is the highest, most beautiful form of love. In return, you will receive untold peace and happiness. (Robert Muller)

- ❖ Thus, it is written, that the Messiah is to suffer and to rise from the dead on the third day, and that repentance and forgiveness of sins is to be proclaimed in his name to all nations, beginning from Jerusalem. (Luke 24:46-47, NRSV)

- ❖ When a deep injury is done to us, we never recover until we forgive. (Alan Paton, author of *Cry, the Beloved Country*)

- ❖ Forgiving is an act of mercy toward an offender. We are no longer controlled by angry feelings toward this person. (Robert D. Enright, PhD, author of *Forgiveness Is a Choice*)

- But if you do not forgive others, neither will your Father forgive your trespasses. (Matt. 6:15, NRSV)

- The recompense for an injury is an injury equal thereto (in degree): but if a person forgives and makes reconciliation, his reward is due from Allah: for Allah loveth not those who do wrong. (Arabic Quran, Surah 42:40)

- Our capacity to make peace with another person and with the world depends very much on our capacity to make peace with ourselves. (Thich Nhat Hanh)

- You know you have forgiven someone when he or she has harmless passage through your mind. (Rev. Karyl Huntley)

- Forgiveness is the release of all hope for a better past. (Alexa Young)

- Anger loses its power over us when we forgive those who hurt us. (Rafael Murillo Paniagua, Mexico, D. F., Mexico)

- In the long run, our growth in forgiveness is a part of our growth in faith. (L. William Countryman)

- We must exercise the same forgiveness for others that we expect to receive from God. (Kamau Ramsey in *Mental Morsels for the Soul*)

- Forgiveness is the scent that the rose leaves on the heel that crushes it. (Anonymous)

- Forgiveness does not change the past, but it does enlarge the future. (Paul Boese)

- Never does the human soul appear so strong as when it foregoes revenge and dares to forgive an injury. (E. H. Chapin)

- To be wronged is nothing unless you continue to remember it.(Confucius)

- If we confess our sins, he who is faithful and just will forgive us our sins and cleanse us from all unrighteousness. If we say that we have not sinned, we make him a liar, and his word is not in us. (1 John 1:9-10, NRSV)

- Life is an adventure in forgiveness. (Norman Cousins)

- Reason to rule, mercy to forgive: The first is law, the last prerogative. (John Dryden)

- Little vicious minds abound with anger and revenge and are incapable of feeling the pleasure of forgiving their enemies. (Earl of Chesterfield)

- In him we have redemption through his blood, the forgiveness of our trespasses, according to the riches of his grace. (Eph. 1:7)

- Forgiveness is better than revenge, for forgiveness is the sign of a gentle nature, but revenge is the sign of a savage nature. (Epictetus)

- Forgiveness is the sweetest revenge. (Isaac Friedman)

- Keeping score of old scores and scars, getting even and one-upping, always makes you less than you are. (Malcolm Forbes)

- If one by one we counted people out for the least sin, it wouldn't take us long to get so we had no one left to live with. For, to be social is to be forgiving. (Robert Frost)

- ❖ The weak can never forgive. Forgiveness is the attribute of the strong. (Mahatma Gandhi)

- ❖ If we practice and eye for an eye and a tooth for a tooth, soon the whole world will be blind and toothless. (Mahatma Gandhi)

- ❖ Forgiveness is the answer to the child's dream of a miracle by which what is broken is made whole again, what is soiled is again made clean. (Dag Hammarskjold)

- ❖ Forgiveness breaks the chain of causality because he who forgives you out of love takes upon himself the consequences of what you have done. Forgiveness, therefore, always entails a sacrifice. (Dag Hammarskjold)

- ❖ A winner rebukes and forgives; a loser is too timid to rebuke and too petty to forgive. (Sidney J. Harris)

- ❖ He that cannot forgive others, breaks the bridge over which he himself must pass if he would ever reach heaven; for everyone has need to be forgiven. (George Herbert)

- ❖ Forgiveness is not an occasional act. It is a permanent attitude. (Martin Luther King)

- ❖ Bear with one another and, if anyone has a complaint against another, forgive each other; just as the Lord has forgiven you, so you also must forgive. (Col. 3:13, NRSV)

- ❖ One of the secrets of a long and fruitful life is to forgive everybody everything every night before you go to bed. (Ann Landers)

- ❖ One pardons to the degree that one loves. (Francois de La Rochefoucauld)

- He who has not forgiven an enemy has never yet tasted one of the most sublime enjoyments of life. (Lauter)

- Forgiveness unleashes joy. It brings peace. It washes the slate clean. It sets all the highest values of love in motion. In a sense, forgiveness is Christianity at its highest level. (John MacArthur)

- Forgiveness is the oil of relationships. (Josh McDowell) Forgiveness is the economy of the heart . . . forgiveness saves the expense of anger, the cost of hatred and the waste of spirits. (Hannah More)

- To forgive is the highest, most beautiful form of love. In return, you will receive untold peace and happiness. (Robert Muller)

- It is not "forgive and forget" as if nothing wrong had ever happened, but 'forgive and go forward,' building on the mistakes of the past and the energy generated by reconciliation to create a new future. (Carolyn Osiek)

- God forgives us. Who am I not to forgive? (Alan Paton)

- It is in pardoning that we are pardoned. (Saint Francis of Assisi)

- In our society, forgiveness is often seen as weakness. People who forgive those who have hurt them or their family are made to look as if they really don't care about their loved ones. But forgiveness is tremendous strength. It is the action of someone who refuses to be consumed by hatred and revenge. (Helen Prejean)

- All religions stress the power of forgiveness, and this power is never more deeply felt than when someone is dying. Through forgiving and being forgiven, we purify ourselves of the darkness of what we have done, and prepare ourselves most completely for the journey through death. (Sogyal Rinpoche)

- ❖ The secret of forgiving everything is to understand nothing. (George Bernard Shaw)

- ❖ It is a very delicate job to forgive a man, without lowering him in his own estimation, and yours too. (Henry Wheeler Shaw)

- ❖ Only the brave know how to forgive; it is the most refined and generous pitch of virtue human nature can arrive at. (Laurence Sterne)

- ❖ Genuine forgiveness is participation, reunion overcoming the powers of estrangement . . . We cannot love unless we have accepted forgiveness, and the deeper our experience of forgiveness is the greater is our love. (Paul Tillich)

- ❖ In forgiving, people are not being asked to forget. On the contrary, it is important to remember, so that we should not let such atrocities happen again. Forgiveness does not mean condoning what has been done. It means taking what happened seriously . . . drawing out the sting in the memory that threatens our entire existence. (Bishop Desmond Tutu)

- ❖ The things that two people in love do to each other they remember. And if they stay together, it is not because they forget, it is because they forgive. (from the movie *IndecentProposal*)

- ❖ Why can we remember the tiniest detail that has happened to us, and not remember how many times we have told it to the same persons? (Francois de La Rochefoucauld)

- ❖ The remarkable thing is that we really love our neighbor as ourselves: we do unto others as we do unto ourselves. We hate others when we hate ourselves. We are tolerant toward others when we tolerate ourselves. We forgive others when we forgive ourselves. We are prone to sacrifice others when we are ready to sacrifice ourselves. (Eric Hoffer)

- Repentance is another name for aspiration. (Henry Ward Beecher)

- In the Bible it says they asked Jesus how many times you should forgive, and he said 70 times 7. Well, I want you all to know that I'm keeping a chart. (Hillary Rodman Clinton)

- It is very easy to forgive others their mistakes; it takes more grit and gumption to forgive them for having witnessed your own. (Jessamyn West)

- Wrongs are often forgiven, but contempt never is. Our pride remembers it forever. (Lord Chesterfield)

- We read that we ought to forgive our enemies; but we do not read that we ought to forgive our friends. (Sir Francis Bacon)

- Forgive, O Lord, my little jokes on Thee And I'll forgive Thy great big one on me. (Robert Frost)

- Forgiveness is freeing up and putting to better use the energy once consumed by holding grudges, harboring resentments, and nursing unhealed wounds. It is rediscovering the strengths we always had and relocating our limitless capacity to understand and accept other people and ourselves. (Sidney and Suzanne Simon)

- As I rejected amnesty, so I reject revenge. I ask all Americans who ever asked for goodness and mercy in their lives, whoever sought forgiveness for their trespasses, to join in rehabilitating all the casualties of the tragic conflict of the past. (Gerald R. Ford)

- As long as you don't forgive, who and whatever it is will occupy rent-free space in your mind. (Isabelle Holland)

- For my part I believe in the forgiveness of sin and the redemption of ignorance. (Adlai E. Stevenson)

- Nothing worth doing is completed in our lifetime, Therefore, we are saved by hope.

- Nothing true or beautiful or good makes complete sense in any immediate context of history; Therefore, we are saved by faith.

- Nothing we do, however virtuous, can be accomplished alone.
- Therefore, we are saved by love.
- No virtuous act is quite a virtuous from the standpoint of our friend or foe as from our own. Therefore, we are saved by the final form of love which is forgiveness. (Reinhold Neibuh

- It is easier to forgive an enemy than to forgive a friend. (William Blake)

- The Forgiveness Bath: It's for giving away any anger you might harbor. It's for giving the person you love another chance and giving in to the love that keeps us afloat. Bathe one another with a sponge, washing away earlier deeds or words that hurt . . . . Let this bath of forgiveness cleanse you and make you happier. Let it strengthen your love and your soul. (*TheNewlywedBathBook* by Cynthia Good and Elizabeth O'Dowd)

- Unforgiveness is the poison we drink hoping that the other person will get sick. (Unknown)

❖ Unforgiveness is emotional *bondage* that consumes minds with memories of *offenses*, distorts emotions with *revenge*, and fills hearts with churning unrest. (Charles Stanley)

❖ People are often unreasonable, irrational, and self-centered; Forgive them **anyway**.

If you are kind, people may accuse you of selfish, ulterior motives; Be kind **anyway**.

If you are successful, you will win some unfaithful friends and some genuine enemies; Succeed **anyway**.

If you are honest and sincere people may deceive you; Be honest and sincere **anyway**.

What you spend years creating, others could destroy overnight; Create **anyway**.

If you find serenity and happiness, some may be jealous; Be happy **anyway**.

The good you do today will often be forgotten. Do good **anyway**.

Give the best you have and it may never be enough; Give your best **anyway**.

In the final analysis, it is between you and God; It was never between you and them **anyway**. (*WordsfromMotherTheresa*)

Endnotes

1. Matt. 6:9-13.
2. Matt. 6:14-15.
3. Dalai Lama and Victor Chan, *The Wisdom of Forgiveness: Intimate Conversations and Journeys* (New York, NY: Riverhead Books, 2004), 73.
4. SatguruSivayaSubramuniyaswami, "Forgiving Others Is Good for Your Health: Hindu Dharma implores us to let go of grudges, resentment and especially self-contempt" in *Hinduism Today* (1997), http://www. hinduismtoday.com/archives/1997/11/1997-11-04.shtml (accessed September 29, 2008).
5. Gary R. Collins, *Christian Counseling: A Comprehensive Guide* (Nashville, TN: Thomas Nelson Publishers, 2007), 804.
6. Gary R. Collins, *Christian Counseling: A Comprehensive Guide* (Nashville, TN: Thomas Nelson Publishers, 2007), 804-805.
7. Gary R. Collins, *Christian Counseling: A Comprehensive Guide* (Nashville, TN: Thomas Nelson Publishers, 2007), 810-811.
8. Heb. 11:6.
9. O. Carl Simonton, Stephanie Matthews-Simonton, and James L. Creighton, *Forgiving Old Hurts: Getting Well Again* (New York, NY: Bantam Books, 1981), 150-151.
10. Edward M. Hallowell, *Dare to Forgive* (Deerfield Beach, FL: Health Communications, Inc., 2004), 43-44.
11. Edward M. Hallowell, *Dare to Forgive* (Deerfield Beach, FL: Health Communications, Inc., 2004), 43-44.
12. Robert D. Enright, *Forgiveness Is a Choice: A Step-by-Step Process for Resolving Anger and Restoring Hope* (Washington, DC: American Psychological Association, 2001).
13. Robert D. Enright and Richard P. Fitzgibbons, *Helping Clients Forgive: An Empirical Guide for Resolving Anger and Restoring Hope*

(Washington, DC: American Psychological Association, 2001), 101-115.
14. Robert D. Enright and Richard P. Fitzgibbons, *Helping Clients Forgive: An Empirical Guide for Resolving Anger and Restoring Hope* (Washington, DC: American Psychological Association, 2001), 157.
15. Johann Christoph Arnold, *Why Forgive?* (Farmington, PA: The Plough Publishing House, 2000), 5-6.
16. Mark 11:25-26.
17. Col. 3:13.
18. Bill Clinton, *My Life* (New York, NY: Alfred A. Knopf Publishers, 2004), 105.
19. Joe Katina, "The Katinas," *http://www.thekatinas.com/index.php?content=bio* (accessed March 1, 2009).
20. Don Baker, *Beyond Forgiveness: The Healing Touch of Church Discipline* (Portland, OR: Multnonah Press, 1984), 95-98.
21. Gary R. Collins, *Christian Counseling: A Comprehensive Guide* (Nashville, TN: Thomas Nelson Publishers, 2007), 170-171.
22. Grace Ketterman and David Hazard, *When You Can't Say "I Forgive You": Breaking the Bonds of Anger and Hurt* (Colorado Springs, CO: Navpress, 2000), 65.
23. Grace Ketterman and David Hazard, *When You Can't Say "I Forgive You": Breaking the Bonds of Anger and Hurt* (Colorado Springs, CO: Navpress, 2000), 70-71.
24. Charles Stanley, *Put the Past Behind You and Give The Gift of Forgiveness* (1991), 16-22.
25. Grace Ketterman and David Hazard, *When You Can't Say "I Forgive You": Breaking the Bonds of Anger and Hurt* (Colorado Springs, CO: Navpress, 2000), 69-72.
26. Colin C. Tipping, *Radical Forgiveness: Making Room for the Miracle*, 2nd ed. (Northboro, MA: Quest Publishing & Distribution, 2002), 45.
27. 1 John 1:9.
28. R. T. Kendall, *Total Forgiveness* (Lake Mary, FL: Charisma House, A Strang Company, 2002), 134-135.
29. R. T. Kendall, *Total Forgiveness* (Lake Mary, FL: Charisma House, A Strang Company, 2002), 135-136.
30. Gal. 6:2.

31. Rom. 13:8.
32. Gal. 6:2.
33. Gary R. Collins, *Christian Counseling: A Comprehensive Guide* (Nashville, TN: Thomas Nelson Publishers, 2007), 188-190.
34. Ps. 51:4.
35. Elisabeth Wetsch, *Serial Killer True Crime Library: Marion Albert Pruett* (2005), http://www.crimezzz.net/serialkillers/P/PRUETT_marion_albert.php (accessed March 27, 2009).
36. The Place for Vengeance. *US News & World Report.* (1997), http://www.prodeathpenalty.com/vengeance.htm (accessed March 2, 2009).
37. MichaelDonald, http://www.spartacus.schoolnet.co.uk/USAdonaldD.htm.
38. Matt. 26:40-42.
39. Matt. 5:45.
40. Mahatma Gandhi, *Quotation #36366 from Classic Quotes: Indian Political and Spiritual Leader, 1869-1948,* http://www.quotationspage.com/ quote/36366.html (accessed February 15, 2009).
41. 1 John 4:20.
42. Stephen Grunlan and Daniel Lambrides, *Healing Relationships: A Christian's Manual for Lay Counseling* (Eugene, OR: Wipf & Stock Publishers), 106-107.

Bibliography

Arnold, Johann Christoph. 2014. *Why forgive?* Farmington, PA: The Plough Publishing House.

Baars, Conrad W. 2009. *Feeling and healing your emotions.* Gainesville, FL: Logo International.

Baker, Don. 1984. *Beyond forgiveness: the healing touch of church discipline.* Portland, OR: Multnonah Press.

Bank, Stephen R., and Michael D. Kahn. 1997. *The sibling bond.* New York, NY: Harper Collins Publishers.

Bloch, Douglas. 1990. *Words that heal: affirmations and meditations for daily living.* New York, NY: Bantam Books.

Bolden, Tonya. 1999. *Forgive or forget: never underestimate the power of forgiveness.* New York, NY: Harper Collins Publishers.

Borysenko, Joan, and Miroslav Borysenko. 1994. *The power of the mind to heal.* Carlsbad, California: Hay House, Inc.

Collins, Gary R. 2007. *Christian counseling: a comprehensive guide.* Nashville, TN: Thomas Nelson Publishers.

Dalai Lama and Victor Chan. 2004. *The wisdom of forgiveness: intimate conversations and journeys.* New York, New York: Riverhead Books, Penguin Group.

Enright, Robert D. 2001. *Forgiveness is a choice: a step-by-step process for resolving anger and restoring hope.* Washington, DC: American Psychological Association.

Finney, Charles G. *Lectures to Professing Christians, Lecture IV. 1836: Reproof A Christian Duty,* http://www.gospeltruth.net/1836LTPC/lptc04_reproof_duty.htm (accessed March 20, 2009).

Foster, Richard J. 2018. *Celebration of discipline: the path to spiritual growth.* San Francisco, CA: Harper Collins Publishers.

Gandhi, Mahatma. *Quotation #36366 from Classic Quotes: Indian political and Spiritual Leader,* http://www.quotationspage.com/quote/36366.html (accessed February 15, 2009).

God's awesome promises: for teens and friends. Dallas, TX: Word Publishing, 1995.

Grosskopf, Barry. 1999. *Forgive your parents, heal yourself: how understanding your painful legacy can transform your life.* New York, NY: The Free Press, Division of Simon & Schuster, Inc.

Hallowell, Edward M. 2004. *Dare to forgive.* Deerfield Beach, FL: Health Communications, Inc.

Harrar, Sari, and Julia Vantine. 1999. *Extraordinary togetherness: a woman's guide to love, sex, and intimacy.* Emmaus, PA: Rodale Books.

Jones, Robert D. 2000. *Forgiveness: I just can't forgive myself!* Phillipsburg, NJ: P & R Publishing.

Kendall, R. T. 2002. *Total forgiveness.* Lake Mary, FL: Charisma House, A Strang Company.

Ketterman, Grace, and David Hazard. 2000. *When you can't say "I forgive you": breaking the bonds of anger and hurt.* Colorado Springs, CO: NavPress Publishing Group.

Klagsbrun, Francine. 1992. *Mixed feelings: love, hate, rivalry, and reconciliation among brothers and sisters.* New York: Bantam Books.

Laney, C. 2010. *A guide to church discipline: God's loving plan for restoring believers to fellowship with himself and with the body of Christ.* Eugene, OR: Wipf and Stock Publishers.

May, Rollo. 1969. *Love and will.* New York, NY: W. W. Norton & Company, Inc.

Miller, D. Patrick. 1999. *A little book of forgiveness: challenges and meditations for anyone with something to forgive.* Berkeley, CA: Fearless Books.

Miller, Ella May. 1977. *The peacemakers: how to find peace and share it.* Old Tappan, NJ: Fleming H. Revell Company.

Nieder, John, and Thomas M. Thompson. 2010. *Forgive and love again: healing wounded relationships.* Eugene, OR: Harvest House Publishers.

Norberg, Tilda. 2002/ *Ashes transformed: healing from trauma - 43 stories of faith.* Nashville, TN: Upper Room Books.

Sanders, Randolph K., ed. 2013. *Christian counseling ethics: a handbook for therapists, pastors & counselors.* Downers Grove, IL: Intervarsity Press Academic.

Schuller, Robert H. 1989. *Believe in the God who believes in you: the ten commandments, a divine design for dignity.* Nashville, TN: Thomas Nelson Publishers.

Smedes, Lewis B. 1997. *The art of forgiving: when you need to forgive and don't know how.* New York, NY: Ballantine Books.

Stanley, Charles. 1991. *Put the Past Behind You and Give The Gift of Forgiveness.* Nashville, TN: Thomas Nelson Publishers.

Stein, J., and Urdang, L., ed. 1966. *The Random House dictionary of the English language: the unabridged edition.* New York: Random House, Inc.

Subramuniyaswami, SatguruSivaya. 1997. "Forgiving Others Is Good for Your Health: Hindu Dharma implores us to let go of grudges, resentment and especially self-contempt" in *Hinduism Today*, http://www.hinduismtoday.com/archives/1997/11/1997-11-04.shtml (accessed September 29, 2008).

Tipping, Colin C. 2002. *Radical forgiveness: making room for the miracle.* Marietta, GA: Global Thirteen Publications, Inc.

Twelve steps and twelve traditions. 2003. New York, NY: Alcoholics Anonymous World Services, Inc.

www.ingramcontent.com/pod-product-compliance
Lightning Source LLC
Chambersburg PA
CBHW021105080526
44587CB00010B/392